AGENTS

The FBI and GPU Infiltration of the Trotskyist Movement

Eric London

Mehring Books
Oak Park, Michigan
2018

© 2019 Mehring Books
www.mehring.com
Published by Mehring Books
P.O. Box 48377
Oak Park, MI 48237
Printed in the United States of America
978-1-893638-85-3

Cover photos: (Top) Sylvia Callen, Joseph Hansen; (Bottom) Leon Trotsky
Cover design: Kevin Reed

Library of Congress Cataloging-in-Publication Data

Names: London, Eric, 1990- author.
Title: Agents : the FBI and GPU infiltration of the Trotskyist movement / Eric London.
Description: Oak Park, Michigan : Mehring Books Inc., [2019] | Includes bibliographical
  references and index.
Identifiers: LCCN 2019002649 (print) | LCCN 2019010699 (ebook) | ISBN
  9781893638860 () | ISBN 9781893638853 (alk. paper)
Subjects: LCSH: Socialist Workers Party--History. | Communism--United States--History--
  20th century. | United States. Federal Bureau of Investigation. | Soviet Union.
  Obyedinennoe gosudarstvennoe politicheskoe upravlenie. | Espionage--United States--
  History--20th century. | Espionage--Soviet Union--History. | Franklin, Sylvia. | Trotsky,
  Leon, 1879-1940--Assassination.
Classification: LCC JK2391.S67 (ebook) | LCC JK2391.S67 .L66 2019 (print) |
  DDC 324.2/175--dc23
LC record available at https://lccn.loc.gov/2019002649

Contents

Dedication

Tom Henehan: 1951–1977

This book is dedicated to Tom Henehan,
martyr of the Fourth International,
who was assassinated on October 16, 1977.

Introduction

The political assassination of Leon Trotsky in Mexico City on August 20, 1940 was the culmination of the terror unleashed by the Soviet Stalinist regime against the entire generation of Marxist politicians, workers, and intellectuals who had been in the vanguard of the October 1917 Revolution that overthrew capitalism in Russia. The murder of Trotsky, the greatest representative of this generation, dealt a staggering blow to the international socialist movement. Its tragic impact on the political consciousness and orientation of the working class, and, consequently, on the prospects for socialist revolution, was to be felt for decades. For this reason, Trotsky's assassination ranks among the most significant and sinister political crimes of the twentieth century.

In the months prior to the attack, Ramon Mercader (alias Frank Jacson), an agent of the Stalinist secret police, the GPU, had ingratiated himself into Trotsky's compound where the leader of the Russian Revolution had been living in exile since January 1937. Mercader entered the compound and met with Trotsky in his office, alone. Mercader pulled out the alpenstock he had hidden in his raincoat and used it. Trotsky died the next day at the age of sixty.

Despite the efforts of the Kremlin bureaucracy and its international syndicate of political lackeys to conceal the assassin's identity and sponsors, there was no doubt of Stalin's role. In the pages of the *Militant*, the newspaper of the Socialist Workers Party (SWP), the Trotskyist movement pointed the finger at Stalin and his global murder operation. In the years prior, this same network of agents had succeeded in killing a significant part of the leadership

5

of the Fourth International, including Leon Sedov, Trotsky's eldest son and leader of the Fourth International in Europe; Rudolf Klement, the Secretary of the Fourth International; and Erwin Wolf, one of Trotsky's secretaries. The Stalinists also murdered Ignatz Reiss, who had defected from the GPU and declared his support for the Fourth International. These assassinations were prepared by a network of agents operating across the world, the aim of which was the liquidation of Trotsky and the Trotskyist movement.

In the weeks and years that followed Trotsky's assassination, agents within the SWP—operating on behalf of both the GPU and the American government—continued their work within the party. They transmitted detailed reports and party documents relating to the names, addresses, children, and jobs of members, as well as party finances, internal political disputes, and international correspondence.

The impact of this great crime was compounded by the fact that for thirty-five years—nearly half the period between the assassination and today—practically nothing was known about how the GPU had carried out the murder of Trotsky or how its agents, as well as agents from the US government, continued to operate inside the Socialist Workers Party and the Fourth International.

In May 1975, the International Committee of the Fourth International initiated the first comprehensive investigation by the Trotskyist movement into the 1940 assassination. The findings of this investigation, as it unfolded over the next decade, were published under the title *Security and the Fourth International.* As previously concealed and undisclosed facts gradually emerged, it became clear that the decades-long failure by the Socialist Workers Party (SWP) in the US—which had been principally responsible for the organization and catastrophic failure of Trotsky's security in Coyoacan—to properly investigate Trotsky's murder was not due to a lack of material resources. Rather, the reason was to be found in the infiltration of the SWP by agents of the Stalinist GPU who were in a position to block an investigation. The most significant of these agents—whose activities are the main focus of this volume—were Joseph Hansen and Sylvia Franklin (neé Callen, party name Sylvia Caldwell).

In a 1981 statement written on behalf of the International Committee, David North explained the historical significance of the investigation:

> It is both the continuation and the culmination of the struggle waged by Trotsky, co-leader of the 1917 October Revolution

and founder of the Fourth International, to expose the crimes of Stalinism and rid the international workers' movement for once and for all of its counterrevolutionary legacy. ...

In referring to *Security and the Fourth International* as an "investigation," it must be grasped that this word only partially embraces the full political and historical content of the struggle waged by the International Committee during the last six years. Like Trotsky's exposure of the Moscow Trial frame-ups of 1936–38, it is the highest conscious expression of the objective movement of the working class against the bourgeoisie and all its agencies.[1]

The breadth and depth of the *Security and the Fourth International* investigation was staggering. What was involved was an immense level of investigative work, spanning multiple continents, hundreds of hours of interviews, and thousands of pages of historical documentation.

For the first time, the Trotskyist movement conducted a systematic investigation into the penetration of the movement by agents of the GPU and the US government. Questions were posed which, had they been asked and investigated decades prior, would have prevented significant damage to the movement and its members.

The investigation was a political struggle conducted under fire from an international network of Stalinists and their political allies, who responded with vitriolic hostility to the *Security and the Fourth International* investigation.

The ICFI insisted there was a political explanation for the attacks on *Security and the Fourth International*. To the Pabloites—an international tendency of ex-Trotskyists that capitulated politically to Stalinism—the ICFI's unforgivable "crime" was to bring to light documents exposing the role of the GPU in destabilizing the Trotskyist movement and murdering its leadership.

In its 1978 perspectives document, the Workers League— the Trotskyist movement in the US, formed in 1966 after being expelled from the SWP— made the following appraisal of the political and historical gains achieved through the investigation, which at that time was still underway:

> *Security and the Fourth International* represents nothing less than the reclamation of the whole historical continuity of Bolshevism

---

1. *How the GPU Murdered Trotsky*, (London: New Park Publications, 1981), p. i.

through the Fourth International and the International Committee from the evil grip of Stalinist counter-revolution and falsification. All the lies and distortions and crimes committed by Stalinism against Trotskyism, the political embodiment of the struggle for the world October; all the monstrous acts committed to confuse and disorient generations of workers about the real history of the October Revolution and the role of Trotsky—these have been dealt a blow from which Stalinism and all the agencies of imperialist counter-revolution will never recover.[2]

This evaluation has been borne out. The Stalinist regimes which once ruled over one sixth of the world's surface no longer exist. The Communist Parties that comprised hundreds of millions of members and dominated the labor movements worldwide have collapsed.

But a quarter century after the dissolution of the Soviet Union, popular interest in socialism is on the rise internationally. Among young people in the US and Europe its popularity surpasses capitalism. But it is precisely in a period of renewed upsurge that the political education of workers and youth in the lessons of the past assumes the greatest importance. The study of the *Security and the Fourth International* investigation not only provides vital historical information about the crimes committed against the Trotskyist movement. It also explains and makes clear the critical importance of all matters relating to political security, in the face of the threat posed by the state and its repressive police and intelligence agencies.

The need for vigilance against state infiltration and provocations arises from the political realities of our time. We live in an age of mass surveillance, targeted assassinations, nonstop war, mass deportations, police killings, and CIA torture. The most advanced representatives of the working class recognize that the political and physical independence of the workers movement from agents of the state is a life or death question upon which the fate of the socialist revolution depends.

The essays that comprise this book deal with two crucial and interrelated themes in the history of the Fourth International.

The first essay, "The Smith Act trial and government infiltration of the Trotskyist movement," draws on information gathered from the valuable

---

2. 1978 Workers League Perspectives Document (unpublished), p. 38.

book, *Trotskyists on Trial: Free Speech and Political Persecution Since the Age of FDR*, by Donna T. Haverty-Stacke as well as from the World Socialist Web Site's independent investigation of thousands of pages of trial transcripts, archive material, and previously unavailable FBI records regarding the US government's decision to prosecute twenty-nine members of the American Trotskyist movement for sedition in the run-up to the Second World War.

The second essay, "An 'Exemplary Comrade': The Socialist Workers Party's forty-year-long cover-up of Stalinist spy Sylvia Callen," traces the ICFI's struggle to expose this Stalinist agent. For nearly nine years, Callen had high-level and unrestricted access to the party's most sensitive information. However, when the Socialist Workers Party learned she was an agent, it helped hide her role as a spy within the Trotskyist movement and launched a cover-up that lasted for nearly four decades.

Finally, this volume includes, as an appendix, "An Open Letter to Susan Weissman," in which David North refutes the lying attempt of this long-time apologist for Joseph Hansen to discredit the *Security and the Fourth International* investigation. It should be noted that Ms. Weissman, comfortably ensconced for many decades in academia, never attempted to answer North's exposure of her falsification of the historical record.

These essays would not have been written without the political assistance of David North, the national chairperson of the Socialist Equality Party, who played a leading role in the *Security and the Fourth International* investigation. I am also indebted to Alan Gelfand and John Burton, who discussed with me the development and outcome of the extraordinary legal action brought by Gelfand (who was represented by Burton) against the SWP and the US government, which led to the discovery of critical documents that totally vindicated the *Security and the Fourth International* investigation. Finally, I am grateful to Jeannie Cooper and Heather Jowsey for their indefatigable work in editing and preparing this book for publication, as well as to Jim Brewer for helping compile and arrange the photographs.

The Smith Act Trial and Government Infiltration of the Trotskyist Movement

On December 8, 1941, eighteen Trotskyists were sentenced to prison terms for advocating the overthrow of the US government. This article is based on information gathered from the valuable book, Trotskyists on Trial: Free Speech and Political Persecution since the Age of FDR, *by Donna T. Haverty-Stacke. In addition, the article draws from the World Socialist Web Site's independent investigation of thousands of pages of trial transcripts; SWP archive material; and previously unavailable FBI records brought to light by Haverty-Stacke.*

In 1941, the Roosevelt administration launched one of the most important political trials in the history of the United States, when it charged twenty-nine members of the Socialist Workers Party (SWP) with sedition and conspiracy to overthrow the government. FBI agents raided the party's offices in Minneapolis on June 27 and prosecutors convened a grand jury shortly thereafter. On October 27, the trial began in federal court. Its proceedings lasted more than one month.

The Socialist Workers Party was aligned politically with the Fourth International at the time of the trial. It was singled out for prosecution as the United States prepared to enter the world war in Europe and the Pacific.

Published on the World Socialist Web Site on December 8 and 9, 2016

The defendants used the trial to defend the party's socialist principles to a broad audience. They explained the SWP's opposition to imperialist war from the witness stand and refuted the prosecution's attempt to portray socialist revolution as a conspiratorial coup d'état. They conducted themselves in a courageous and principled manner, with federal prison sentences hanging over their heads. In the 1942 pamphlet, *Socialism on Trial*, the SWP published the trial transcript of SWP National Chairman James P. Cannon's spirited testimony.

On December 1, 1941, the jury found eighteen of the defendants guilty of violating the newly enacted Smith Act, but recommended leniency in sentencing. On December 8, one day after the Japanese attack on Pearl Harbor, the trial judge read the "18" their sentences, which ranged from twelve to sixteen months. On November 22, 1943, the Supreme

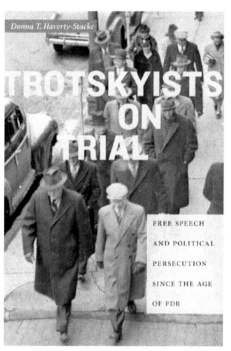

Court refused to take the appeal lodged by the defendants. The next month, the "18" surrendered themselves to federal authorities and began serving their sentences. Despite a national campaign that generated support from thousands of workers and many prominent intellectuals and attorneys, Roosevelt refused to pardon the defendants. Six of the eighteen were released after ten months, and the remaining twelve were released in January 1945 after serving over one year.

This significant event in the history of the socialist movement is the subject of a new book published seventy-five years after the trial by Hunter College Professor Donna Haverty-Stacke. The book, titled *Trotskyists on Trial: Free Speech and Political Persecution since the Age of FDR* (New York University Press, 2015), is a significant work, and its author is to be congratulated on her accomplishment. Haverty-Stacke has not only taken up a subject that has been ignored by academia, she has also brought to light many previously unknown details of the prosecution and its political and legal ramifications.

Haverty-Stacke has undertaken a painstaking review of previously unexamined or unavailable archived material from the Department of Justice and the Federal Bureau of Investigation. This material has been largely unexplored by academics, who have all but ignored (with the notable exception of Bryan Palmer's biography of James P. Cannon and his history of the 1934 Minneapolis General Strike) the significant role of Trotskyism in American political life.

Haverty-Stacke's book provides a wealth of new information regarding the extent of the penetration of the Trotskyist movement by FBI agents and informants. She presents the discussions taking place within the Roosevelt administration as it prepared the first peacetime sedition prosecution since those following the passage of the Alien and Sedition Acts of 1798. She addresses the legal issues involved in the trial, the appeal before the Eighth Circuit Court of Appeals, and the case's precedential role in laying the foundation for further anti-communist trials in the 1940s and 1950s. She begins by providing the backdrop to the trial and biographical sketches of the defendants.

The selection of the defendants

The Socialist Workers Party was a major force within the American left. This was the product not only of its leadership of key strikes during the 1930s,

1941: Fourteen of the eighteen SWP members convicted under the Smith Act. Back row, left-to-right: Farrell Dobbs, Harry DeBoer, Edward Palmquist, Clarence Hamel, Emil Hansen, Oscar Coover, Jake Cooper; Front row, left-to-right: Max Geldman, Felix Morrow, Albert Goldman, James Cannon, Vincent Dunne, Carl Skoglund, Grace Carlson

James P. Cannon (center) with Max Eastman (left) and "Big" Bill Haywood (right) in the Soviet Union, 1922

but also, and above all, its identification with the political conceptions of Leon Trotsky. His enormous stature as leader, along with Vladimir Lenin, of the 1917 October Revolution; implacable opponent of the Stalinist degeneration of the Soviet Union; and one of the greatest writers of his time made Trotsky, even in exile, a major presence in world politics. Even after his assassination in August 1940, the lasting influence of Trotsky's ideas was feared by his enemies among the Stalinists, the fascists and the "democratic" imperialists. First and foremost among those in the latter category was the US government under the leadership of President Franklin Delano Roosevelt.

There were two sets of defendants amongst the twenty-nine charged: the party's political leadership based in the SWP's national headquarters in New York City, and the SWP's representatives in Minneapolis, Minnesota who occupied positions of leadership in the region's Teamster's union, Local 544.

The first group of defendants consisted of long-standing leaders of the SWP, professional revolutionaries whose principles were forged in the class struggles of the early twentieth century.

Haverty-Stacke notes that foremost among these defendants was James P. Cannon, the national chairman of the SWP and the founder of Trotskyism in the United States. Born in 1890 in Rosedale, Kansas, Cannon read Trotsky's critique of Stalinist policies while attending the Sixth Congress of the Communist International, held in Moscow in 1928. Upon returning to

Albert Goldman advises Trotsky during a session of the Dewey Commission in Mexico

the United States, he declared his agreement with Trotsky. Expelled from the Communist Party, he founded the American section of the Left Opposition and established contact with Trotsky.

Felix Morrow, born in 1906 in New York City, was an SWP political committee member and revolutionary journalist who wrote for the party press. He was respected as the author of the book *Revolution and Counter-Revolution in Spain.* At trial, the prosecution emphasized Morrow's position on the editorial board of *Fourth International,* the party's theoretical journal.

Albert Goldman, another leading figure in the SWP, migrated to the United States from Belorussia at the age of seven in 1904. Goldman was best known for serving as Leon Trotsky's attorney before the Dewey Commission of Inquiry's hearings on the Stalinist show trials in 1937. The Roosevelt administration sought the indictment of these three men because their political and, in the case of Cannon and Goldman, personal association, was central to establishing, in accordance with the law, a conspiracy to overthrow the government. One significant omission from the list of defendants was Joseph Hansen, who had served as Trotsky's secretary for three years, from 1937 until 1940. His absence from the list will be discussed below.

The second group of defendants served in the SWP leadership in Minneapolis, where the party's direction of the Teamsters union had established the Trotskyist movement as a significant political force commanding the respect of thousands of workers. Many of the Trotskyist defendants had personally led the victorious 1934 truckers' general strike in the Twin Cities and fought to recruit two hundred thousand members to the union across the Midwestern states.

Haverty-Stacke describes the history of the communist movement in the area, noting how Minneapolis became a center of support for the Left Opposition after the Stalinist Communist Party expelled the Trotskyists from the party in 1928: "Along with him [Cannon] went other future Smith Act defendants in Minneapolis, including Vincent Dunne, Carl Skoglund, and Oscar Coover."[1]

Vincent R. Dunne arrested during National Guard raid on Local 574 strike headquarters in 1934

In the years following the general strike, the national Teamsters union under the leadership of close Roosevelt confidant Daniel Tobin unsuccessfully sought to purge Local 544 (and its predecessor, Local 574) of its Trotskyist leadership, employing the most vicious anti-communist propaganda.

In the weeks before the government initiated its prosecution, Local 544 was engaged in a renewed political battle over control of the Minneapolis Teamsters union. When Tobin and the Teamsters leadership launched a new

---

1. Haverty-Stacke, Donna T., *Trotskyists on Trial: Free Speech and Political Persecution since the Age of FDR.* (New York: New York University Press, 2015), p. 11.

attempt to remove the Trotskyists from their positions, in part due to the SWP's opposition to US entry into World War II, thousands of truck drivers voted to abandon the American Federation of Labor (AFL) and re-certify the local with the Congress of Industrial Organizations (CIO).

The Minneapolis defendants had played key roles in the decertification efforts. Vincent Dunne was one of them, and he was joined in the defendants dock by his brothers Miles and Grant. All three had led the general strike alongside Skoglund. Grant was unable to bear the immense pressure of the prosecution and took his own life on October 4.

Harry DeBoer, a truck driver, was active during the general strike and was shot by the police. A key member of the SWP in Minneapolis, he visited Trotsky in Mexico City several years later.

Grace Carlson was a social service worker and former professor at the University of Minnesota who ran as the party's candidate for US Senate on an anti-war platform in 1940, garnering over 8,500 votes.

Jake Cooper, also from Minneapolis, served as Trotsky's guard at Coyoacan for a four-month period in 1940.

Farrell Dobbs, a former coal yard worker, was appointed national labor secretary of the SWP in 1939 after organizing strikes of thousands of truck drivers in the Midwest. Other Minneapolis-based defendants who were ultimately convicted included Max Geldman, Clarence Hamel, Emil Hansen, Carlos Hudson, Karl Kuehn, Edward Palmquist, and Oscar Schoenfeld.

The editorial board of the party's *Fourth International* magazine wrote in July 1941, after the indictment list was published: "Yes, there is a profound logic in the fact that these persecutions and prosecutions are instigated by the Gestapo-FBI at this time and in this place and against the specifically-designated victims."[2]

This logic would play out at trial when the prosecution submitted evidence of the close connection several of the defendants had to Leon Trotsky in Mexico. The visits of Cooper, DeBoer, Vincent Dunne, Cannon and Dobbs to Mexico were presented as evidence of an anti-government conspiracy, as was Goldman's close relation to Trotsky in the years preceding the trial. The government selected each "specifically-designated victim" with an eye to proving that a conspiratorial connection existed between Trotsky and the SWP's alleged preparations for social revolution.

---

2. The Editors, ed. "The FBI-Gestapo Attack on the Socialist Workers Party," *Fourth International* 2.6 (1941), p. 166. Available: https://www.marxists.org/history/etol/news-pape/fi/vol02/no06/v02n06-w13-jul-1941.pdf

The Smith Act

The defendants were charged with two criminal counts. The first of the two charges against the twenty-nine defendants was "unlawful conspiracy from and before July 18, 1938, to date of the indictment [June 23, 1941] ... to destroy by force the government of the United States" in violation of 18 US Code Section 6, a Civil War-era statute written to suppress the slaveholders rebellion.[3]

The second charge alleged that those indicted "advised insubordination in the armed forces with intent and distributed literature to the same effect," and "knowingly and willfully would, and they did, advocate, abet, advise and teach the duty, necessity, desirability and propriety of overthrowing and destroying the government of the United States by force and violence" in violation of the 1940 Alien Registration Act, also known as the "Smith Act" after the bill's congressional sponsor, Howard Smith (Democrat of Virginia).[4]

Haverty-Stacke describes in detail the anti-communist predecessors to the Smith Act, from the criminal syndicate statutes of the "Red Scare"-era following World War I to the 1938 House Committee Investigating Un-American Activities, established by Texas Democratic Congressman Martin Dies.

The Smith Act's criminal sedition sections made it a crime to advocate, write or organize for the overthrow of the US government, punishable by a jail term of up to twenty years. Its sections relating to immigration required the immediate registration of five million immigrants, nine hundred thousand of whom were soon after categorized as "enemy aliens" subject to internment and/or immediate deportation. This same law, used to target socialists and communists, was also used to intern 120,000 Japanese-Americans on the West Coast during the war. In contrast to efforts to portray Roosevelt as a defender of democratic rights, he was at the very center of the intensification of repressive police measures.

The Communist Party, which took its political instructions from Moscow and the Soviet secret police, the GPU, wholeheartedly supported the Smith Act prosecution of the Trotskyists (as it later supported the internment of Japanese-Americans). CP leader Milton Howard supported the prosecution of the "fascist fifth column" on the grounds that the defendants "deserve no

---

3. Haverty-Stacke, p. 77.
4. Ibid.

more support from labor and friends of national security than do the Nazis."[5] Speaking in Minneapolis, Stalinist functionary Robert Minor said the Roosevelt administration should follow the example set by Moscow [during the Great Terror of 1936–39] in dealing with the American Trotskyists.[6]

Howard W. Smith, Democrat of Virginia

The passage of the Smith Act marked a drastic expansion of the surveillance powers of the state, aimed at socialist groups operating in the United States. Haverty-Stacke points out that in 1939, "Three days before the House sent H.R. 5138, now known as the Alien Registration Bill, to the Senate, President Roosevelt issued a secret order 'placing all domestic investigations [of espionage, counterespionage, and sabotage] under the FBI, Military Intelligence Division, and Office of Naval Intelligence,' with the FBI as the central coordinating agency."[7]

As early as 1936, FBI Director J. Edgar Hoover was sending Roosevelt reports on "domestic subversives," which included the Trotskyist leadership.[8] Hoover continued to pressure the president for the authority to intensify his surveillance, and Roosevelt signed the bill into law on June 29, 1940. Haverty-Stacke writes that by the time the bill became law, the FBI's infiltration of the SWP was already well underway: "By late 1939, both Teamsters Local 544 in Minneapolis and the Socialist Workers Party headquartered in New York became targets of the bureau's investigations."[9]

---

5. Ibid., p. 79.
6. Ibid., p. 108.
7. Ibid., p. 34. (Citing "Confidential Memo for the Secretary of State, the Secretary of the Treasury, the Secretary of War, the Attorney General, the Postmaster General, the Secretary of the Navy and the Secretary of Commerce from President Roosevelt, June 26, 1939, OF 10b, box10, FDRPL").
8. Ibid., p. 41.
9. Ibid., p. 30.

The decision to prosecute

As the US prepared actively for entry into the war, Roosevelt faced the challenge of imposing the type of class discipline needed for the war effort. For the previous twenty-two months, the Stalinist Communist Party of the United States of America (CPUSA) had opposed US involvement in the war in Europe, in keeping with the August 1939 Stalin-Hitler pact. But with the German invasion of the Soviet Union on June 22, 1941, the CPUSA pivoted from opposition to US intervention in the war to full support for the Roosevelt administration's war drive. The Stalinists immediately began transforming their apparatus into a mechanism to police the working class and enforce a nationwide "no strike" policy.

SWP denounces Smith Act prosecution by "American Gestapo"

The Roosevelt administration decided to prosecute the Trotskyists on June 23, 1941, the day after the German invasion of the Soviet Union. With the CPUSA reversing its previous stance, and now become a pro-war party, the SWP became the most significant socialist anti-war party in the United States. The Roosevelt administration was concerned that the movement's principled opposition to imperialist war would make it a pole of attraction for anti-war sentiment in the American working class.

The decision to prosecute followed months of intense discussion at the highest levels of the Department of Justice and the FBI. Haverty-Stacke examines the contentious legal and political problems that confronted the government.

FBI Director J. Edgar Hoover

Hoover was an early advocate of prosecution. But for the Department of Justice and Roosevelt himself, prosecution entailed a series of risks. Leading administration officials such as Solicitor General Francis Biddle were concerned that the prosecution could generate broad opposition, galvanizing the SWP and alienating the Roosevelt administration's liberal base.

In June 1941, Hoover attempted to pressure Roosevelt, claiming that, should the US enter the war, the Socialist Workers Party could "cause a tie-up of materials flowing to and from plants in that vicinity having National Defense contracts."[10] That same month, US Attorneys Victor Anderson and Wendell Berge indicated their support for prosecution.[11] On June 12, Teamsters President Tobin sent Roosevelt a telegram requesting prosecution. Haverty-Stacke writes: "Tobin argued that the Trotskyists, who had succeeded in organizing drivers across the central states, were in a position to disrupt the nation's commercial transportation networks and, if they took advantage of the war crisis, could overthrow the government and set up a socialist state."[12]

The SWP claimed during the trial and in its aftermath that Roosevelt decided to prosecute the SWP as a result of Tobin's June 12 telegram. But this was only partially true. Haverty-Stacke explains:

> Because of this telegram, Tobin has been accused of setting in motion the chain of events that led to the arrest of twenty-nine members of the SWP and Local 544. At the time of those arrests and during the trial, the defense argued that Tobin called in a political favor from Roosevelt and that the president intervened in an internal union dispute, launching the first Smith Act prosecution. This "political debt" argument has survived in varying degrees in the limited scholarly literature on the case and has informed the popular memory of the prosecution within the SWP. The Department of Justice, however, had already been seriously considering such prosecution as early as April 1941, *based on the independent investigation of the FBI dating back to the fall of 1940.*[13] (Emphasis added)

Ultimately, according to Haverty-Stacke, Francis Biddle "made the move in this case largely because of the intelligence he received from the FBI."[14]

---

10. Ibid., p. 62.
11. Ibid., p. 61.
12. Ibid., p. 60.
13. Ibid., p. 61.
14. Ibid., p. 73.

The centrality of Leon Trotsky to the prosecution's case

Though Haverty-Stacke does not focus on this issue in her book, the WSWS investigation of the trial record makes clear that the prosecution's theory of the case is centered on establishing the connection between the SWP defendants and Leon Trotsky. This became the crucial legal issue around which the entire case revolved. Under this theory, Trotsky was the architect, instructor and director of the SWP's activities in Minneapolis and across the country. So central was Trotsky to the prosecution's case that he was listed as a co-conspirator at the grand jury phase, despite the fact that he had been killed the prior August.

The experienced US attorneys from the Department of Justice, aware that a verdict of "not guilty" on both counts would be an immense embarrassment for the administration, laid out a strategy aimed at securing convictions. Their theory of the case revolved around showing the connection between Trotsky and the SWP defendants.

The prosecutors searched for any evidence that tended to show the defendants had met or corresponded with Trotsky or traveled to Mexico City. They submitted evidence of even the slightest connections between the SWP and Trotsky to advance their theory.

In the prosecution's opening argument, the US attorneys claimed that the SWP:

> ... was an instrumentality framed by a man who departed this life in August 1940, by the name of Leon Trotsky, who at the time of his departure, I believe, was in exile in the Republic of Mexico, and that this party was the Trotsky Party, or the party was dedicated to carry into effect the ideas and the plans and the views of Leon Trotsky with respect to the establishment of a government here on earth, and particularly as this refers to the United States of America, and that the program of this party, or the ideas that were basic in this party, represented the views of Leon Trotsky, and those of his contemporary, the first executive head of the Soviet Union, V.I. Lenin, and that their philosophy was that they could reach a solution of all their problems by the establishment of a workers' state... and that the defendants, or a large number of them, with the knowledge of all these defendants here on trial, made trips to Leon Trotsky in Mexico for the purpose of receiving his counsel and guidance and direction

from time to time, not only in furnishing a personal bodyguard and in furnishing protection to Leon Trotsky, for his personal safety, but otherwise contributing to Leon Trotsky and his activities while he was at the outskirts of Mexico City, in Mexico, until the time of his assassination, and that these ideas of Leon Trotsky's are the ideas of the Socialist Workers Party, and so far as the evidence in this case will show, the affirmative and positive ideas of all the defendants upon trial.[15]

This Is Now FBI "Evidence"

This is the picture of Leon Trotsky which FBI agents snatched from the walls of the Minneapolis headquarters of the Socialist Workers Party last week. This is part of the "evidence" which the government will use in its attempt to frame-up leaders of General Drivers Union Local 544-CIO on charges of "seditious conspiracy."

The Militant: "This is now FBI 'evidence'"

Even a single visit to Trotsky in Coyoacan was flaunted by the prosecutors as proof of conspiracy. So brazen were the state prosecutors, that SWP attorney and defendant Albert Goldman raised legal objections to the prosecution's excessive reliance on evidence of SWP visits to Mexico. The government, Goldman claimed, made it seem that visiting Trotsky was itself a conspiratorial act. US Attorney Henry A. Schweinhaut replied:

> The law, I am certain, as counsel knows, with respect to a conspiracy, is that a conspiracy can be accomplished not alone by doing an illegal act but by the doing of, for example, legal acts for an unlawful purpose. The testimony here has already shown and it will be shown again that these men held out Trotsky as their leader. It becomes an important matter to show the association

15. Prosecution's Opening Statement, *US v. Dunne et al.*, pp. 26–27.

of the defendants personally with Trotsky and in doing so it can
be shown what the nature of the association was.[16]

In particular, the prosecution sought to show that Trotsky elaborated
two of the SWP's "conspiratorial" policies—the SWP's proletarian military
policy and the Union Defense Guard.

The proletarian military policy was developed by Trotsky and communicated to the SWP leadership through personal meetings and extensive
correspondence in the years that preceded Trotsky's assassination in August
1940.[17] The proposal for a Union Defense Guard was initiated by Trotsky
for the purpose of defending workers and socialists from attacks by fascist
paramilitary organizations, which had established a presence in Minneapolis.

The prosecution's theory of the case relied on showing (a) that such pro-
grams existed and were being implemented by the SWP in Minneapolis, (b)
that they were conceived of by Trotsky, and (c) that Trotsky's suggestions were
conveyed to the SWP via personal communication with several of the defendants. The US attorneys spent weeks at trial using evidence gathered through
months of investigation to prove each link.

The previously unknown extent of government infiltration of the SWP

Haverty-Stacke's book reveals that by late 1940, the FBI had acquired
extensive knowledge of the SWP's activities and had access to high-level
informants within the party's New York headquarters.

The surveillance of the Trotskyist movement had begun in the mid-
1930s, when the FBI began placing certain party leaders under surveillance.
Haverty-Stacke notes: "The Trotskyists found themselves targets of both the
SDU's [Special Defense Unit's] recommendations and the FBI's Custodial
Detention list. A few of the '18' had already been categorized by Hoover in
the most dangerous grouping—'A1'—before their prosecution."[18]

---

16. *US v. Dunne et al.*, p. 130.

17. For a detailed explanation of the character of the proletarian military policy, see *The Heritage We Defend*, (Oak Park, MI: Mehring Books, 2018), Ch. 6: "Trotsky's Proletarian Military Policy."

18. Haverty-Stacke, p. 153. (Citing J. Edgar Hoover to Special Agent in Charge, New York, June 16, 1942, re. Farrell Dobbs, Internal Security, in Farrell Dobbs's FBI file 100-21226, FOIA, in the author's possession; Joseph Prendergast, Acting Chief SDU, to Wendell Berge, January 31, 1942, and Wendell Berge to J. Edgar Hoover, April 25, 1942 in Farrell Dobbs's FBI

James Bartlett, an ex-SWP member turned-informant (Right), pictured in Mexico with Trotsky and defendant Harold De Boer (Left)

By late 1939, as Haverty-Stacke notes, the FBI had already targeted the SWP in Minneapolis and New York. But even the following year the infiltration was still somewhat primitive. In April 1940, the FBI resorted to paying a janitor at a Chicago event center to retrieve information from trashcans regarding delegates to the SWP congress.

In this period, Haverty-Stacke explains, there were two essential elements to the government infiltration. First, the government obtained informants from a minority faction of Local 574/544 that was opposed to the Trotskyist leadership on an anti-communist basis. James Bartlett, the government's star witness at trial, represented this reactionary element. Second, the government based its infiltration program on the acquisition of informants from within the SWP.

According to Haverty-Stacke, the FBI sought to recruit agents from within the SWP leadership. They attempted to contact and recruit SWP leaders in the months before the Roosevelt administration made the decision to prosecute.

According to the testimony of FBI informant Henry Harris, FBI Agent Thomas Perrin asked Harris to convey an offer to SWP defendant Carl

file 146-7-1355, FOIA, in the author's possession; Chief of SDU to J. Edgar Hoover, February 26, 1942, in Dunne's FBI file 100-18341, and Edward Palmquist's Custodial Detention Card, in Palmquist's FBI file 146-7-1213; J. Edgar Hoover to Chief of SDU, March 31, 1941, in Dunne's FBI file 100-18341).

Skoglund in early 1941.[19] Skoglund, a Swedish-born socialist, was living in the US without proper immigration papers. The FBI offer was for Skoglund to provide information to the FBI in return for impunity and a permanent resolution of his immigration problems. Skoglund refused the offer. A central element of the FBI's infiltration was offering key figures an "impunity" incentive to become informants and aid the prosecution.[20]

FBI Agent Roy Noonan testified that the FBI obtained a major new source of information in the autumn of 1940. Noonan played the role of lead investigator, tasked with overseeing the evidence-gathering operation against the SWP in Minnesota.

US Attorney Schweinhaut and SWP Attorney Albert Goldman questioned Agent Noonan. Noonan noted that by 1941, the FBI "had several investigations of the Socialist Workers Party in their files for the past years."[21]

Schweinhaut asked Noonan when the FBI began its investigation into the SWP defendants and Noonan replied: "[W]e have had several of them in our files in past years, but *in the latter part of 1940*, two or three specifically."[22] (Emphasis added)

On cross-examination, Goldman and Noonan had the following exchange:

> Goldman: And how long before that did the investigation start, as far as you know?
> Noonan: I know that the investigation was being conducted in February and March [1941], and I know that we have had information regarding some of the defendants long before that.
> Goldman: How long before that?
> Noonan: I know we had it in November, 1940.[23]

The November 1940 date corresponds with Haverty-Stacke's finding that the decision to prosecute was "based on the independent investigation of the FBI dating back to the fall of 1940."[24]

---

19. Testimony of Henry Harris, *US v. Dunne et al.*, p. 507.
20. Haverty-Stacke, p. 78.
21. Cross Examination of Agent Roy T. Noonan, *US v. Dunne et al.*, p. 371.
22. Ibid., p. 372.
23. Ibid., p. 371.
24. Haverty-Stacke, p. 61.

After the FBI obtained a higher degree of information regarding the defendants in November 1940, the FBI was able to oversee a vast expansion of its infiltration network. Noonan testified at trial that the surveillance "was intensified in February and March of this year [1941]."[25]

Recently declassified FBI communications show a qualitative development in the FBI's infiltration network from November 1940 to mid-1941. The FBI files include dozens of reports by agents located in Omaha, Kansas City, St. Louis, Minneapolis, Seattle, Los Angeles, Mississippi, New York, New Jersey and elsewhere, quoting from confidential informants. The FBI files from the year 1941 include transcripts of branch meetings and full subscription lists to the party press. The FBI knew how much money each branch was raising and when it was holding meetings. The FBI had full schedules of the national speaking tours before they were publicly announced, as well as minutes from Political Committee meetings. It was aware of who was elected to serve on what national board, including the Control Commission. The FBI had also acquired substantial information about foreign affiliates to the Fourth International, indicating a high degree of infiltration of the New York headquarters.

"By the spring of 1941," Haverty-Stacke writes, "the investigation thus had broadened out beyond the Teamsters in Minneapolis to mesh with the existing investigations of national SWP leaders in New York."[26] By that time, the party's "two most active branches [Minneapolis and New York] remained under heavy FBI surveillance, riddled with *well-placed informants*."[27] (Emphasis added) According to Haverty-Stacke, "The FBI watched the SWP's national headquarters in New York in particular very closely."[28]

Hoover's priority at trial: Preventing the exposure of the SWP informant network

Internal government documents uncovered by Haverty-Stacke also shed light on the qualities Hoover was looking for in an informant. Haverty-Stacke points to a June 1941 conversation between Hoover, Solicitor General Francis Biddle, and US Attorneys Schweinhaut and Wendell Berge. In the

---

25. *US v. Dunne et al.*, pp. 371–372.
26. Haverty-Stacke, p. 50.
27. Ibid., p. 155.
28. Ibid., p. 154. (Citing FBI report 100–413, NYC 10/20/42 and 12/3/42, f. 7, box 108, SWP 146-1-10).

year. Tommy Williams was interviewed by agents of the F.B.I. in this case in February, 1941. He is now dead. I understand he died March 10, 1941.

Cross Examination by Mr. Goldman

There were other books in the St. Paul office which we did not take and of which I did not make a list. I don't remember all of the other books. I don't know whether there were any books dealing with poetry or literature. This investigation started before I came into the St. Paul office. It started in February or March, 1941. We have had information regarding some of the defendants before then. I know we had it in November, 1940.

Q. Do you know that your superior received instructions from Washington after a telegram was sent to Washington by President Tobin of the International to continue the investigation and to get an indictment?

MR. ANDERSON: I object to that as incompetent, irrelevant and immaterial and not proper cross examination.

THE COURT: Sustained. I don't see what difference it makes what this man knew about it. He was directed to go ahead and make the investigation.

MR. GOLDMAN: But the question of investigation and the motives for it --

THE COURT: That is right. He doesn't determine the motives that actuated the investigation.

The witness, continuing:

I talked to about fifty people in the course of my investigation and I would say about 25 of them were members of 544

* * * * * *

-372-

Trial transcript of Agent Roy T. Noonan's testimony, p. 372

course of this discussion, the Department of Justice lawyers suggested the FBI place its own agents in SWP headquarters in New York to gather evidence in preparation for trial.

Schweinhaut was first to propose this plan of action to Hoover. Berge seconded Schweinhaut, writing Hoover in mid-June 1941: "[I]f you think there is information which, from the investigative standpoint, can be best secured by the method you discussed with me on the telephone, you are authorized to order such an investigation," noting that the administration attorneys "agree that it would not amount to entrapment so long as the government agents do not inspire the doing of illegal acts merely for the purpose of getting evidence."[29]

Hoover's response revealingly sheds light on his strategy for infiltrating the SWP. His concerns were two-fold.

Replying to the Justice Department attorneys, he first expressed a fear that FBI agents placed in headquarters for the purpose of gathering evidence for trial could pose a "serious possibility of embarrassment to the Bureau ... if the agent were later used as a witness and required to testify in open court."[30]

In an additional section of his response letter (a section to which Haverty-Stacke does not make reference), Hoover explains that not only was the Justice Department suggestion risky, it would also be ineffective from an information gathering standpoint.

Hoover wrote: "The possibilities of obtaining important evidence in the immediate future through such an arrangement are very doubtful, inasmuch as a new member of the Party would necessarily have to establish himself and satisfy the Party leaders as to his reliability prior to being the recipient of confidential information," and that this would take a "considerable amount of time, probably months."[31]

From these quotations, the following conclusion can be inferred. To Hoover, an informant was valuable insofar as he (a) could be protected from being exposed publicly by testifying at trial, (b) was already operating at the highest levels of the SWP and with the confidence of the SWP leadership, and (c) could provide the FBI with information immediately without the

---

29. Ibid., p. 63. (Citing J. Edgar Hoover to Matthew McGuire, June 25, 1941, f. 2, box 108, SWP 146-1-10; Wendell Burge to Henry Schweinhaut, June 25, 1941, f. 2, box 108, SWP 146-1-10; J. Edgar Hoover to Matthew McGuire, June 25, 1941, f. 2, box 108, SWP 146-1-10).
30. Ibid.
31. J. Edgar Hoover to Matthew McGuire, June 25, 1941, f. 2, box 108, SWP 146-1-10

risks and delays associated with an outside agent ingratiating himself into the party leadership.

This discussion took place in mid-June 1941. Eight months earlier, Hoover had begun personally monitoring discussions between B.E. Sackett, the FBI's chief agent in New York City, and Joseph Hansen, a key leader of the SWP who had served as Trotsky's secretary in Mexico City.

Hansen met all of Hoover's criteria. He had already won the confidence of the party leadership and was in a position to provide "important evidence" to the FBI without delay and with minimal risk of exposure. As the prosecution unfolded over the following months, Hansen's name was almost inexplicably absent from the list of SWP defendants.

Joseph Hansen's secret meetings with the US government

Haverty-Stacke makes use of trial records and newly available FBI records to investigate how the FBI prepared for the prosecution of twenty-nine members of the SWP in the Smith Act trial of 1941.

The material presented by Haverty-Stacke provides a much clearer picture of this key period in the history of the socialist movement. It lends enormous weight to documents uncovered by the International Committee of the Fourth International in 1975 as part of its *Security and the Fourth International* investigation, which revealed that the State Department and FBI held meetings, beginning in September 1940, with a leading figure in the SWP, Joseph Hansen. In the context of the new material published by Haverty-Stacke, one central question arises: Why was Joseph Hansen absent from the list of defendants in the Smith Act trial?

The documents published in the initial *Security and the Fourth International* investigation show that Joseph Hansen established communication with the US government after Trotsky's assassination. Between 1975 and 1978, the investigation raised the question: why would Hansen have been interested in contacting the government, and why did he do so without notifying the SWP leadership? Hansen claimed in *Healy's Big Lie* that he met with the FBI "just once."[32] This was proven to be untrue.

Hansen had spent three years as Trotsky's personal assistant in Coyoacan, Mexico. Of the small handful of Americans residing at Trotsky's compound,

---

32. Hansen, Joseph, "Healy's Big Lie: The Slander Campaign Against Joseph Hansen, George Novack," *Fourth International: Statements and Articles*, (New York: National Education Dept., Socialist Workers Party, 1976), p. 14.

The statement of the International Committee of the Fourth International which appeared in the Bulletin of August 5, 1977

Hansen was the most politically involved and had the closest connections with the leadership of the SWP in the US. Ten days after Trotsky's death on August 21, 1940, Hansen contacted the US Embassy in Mexico City with the hope of opening up a confidential relationship with the US government.

Hansen's meetings were carefully followed by the highest levels of the American government. Figures such as George P. Shaw, Robert McGregor and B.E. Sackett were assigned to lead and follow the investigation. Shaw, a high-ranking State Department diplomat, had worked at the US consulate in Tegucigalpa, Honduras; San Luis Potosi, Mexico; and Ciudad Juarez, Mexico, and was later to serve as ambassador to Nicaragua, El Salvador and

FBI Director J. Edgar Hoover

Paraguay.[33] McGregor served as secretary of the US consulate in Mexico, and Sackett was the special agent in charge of the New York division of the FBI. Within weeks of Hansen's first contact, J. Edgar Hoover was personally monitoring the meetings between Hansen and government officials.

Other officials following Hansen's case included Raymond E. Murphy of the State Department and H.H. Clegg of the FBI. Murphy was a well-connected State Department officer who was later to champion prosecution of suspected spy J. Alger Hiss. Murphy was the State Department official who first made information about Whittaker Chambers available to Congressman Richard M. Nixon of the House Un-American Activities Committee.[34] Clegg was a veteran FBI agent who later served as assistant director of the FBI.[35] Government officials handled the matter with

33. Political Graveyard Entry for George Price Shaw, accessible at http://politicalgrave-yard.com/bio/shaw.html; US State Department History Office of the Historian Entry for George Price Shaw, accessible at https://history.state.gov/departmenthistory/people/shaw-george-price?

34. Morgan, Ted. *A Covert Life: Jay Lovestone: Communist, Anti-Communist, and Spymaster* (New York, New York: Random House, 1999), p. 149.

35. Historical G-Men: "1930s FBI Biographies and More." Entry for H. H. Clegg, accessible at http://historicalgmen.squarespace.com/agents-of-the-30s-biographie/

Joseph Hansen at Trotsky's funeral, Mexico, August, 1940

great delicacy and interest. (See Appendix B for these exchanges.)

A September 1, 1940 letter from US Embassy official George P. Shaw to the State Department includes "a memorandum of a conversation which took place on August 31, 1940, between Consul [Robert G.] McGregor of this office and Mr. Joseph Hansen, secretary to the late Mr. Leon Trotsky."[36]

The memorandum reads: "Mr. Joseph Hansen, secretary to the late Mr. Trotsky, came in on Saturday morning in order to discuss matters connected with the assassination of Mr. Trotsky."[37]

During this first meeting, Hansen provided the government with information surrounding the assassination. At this time, Hansen communicated to the US government that he had met for three months in 1938 with agents of Stalin's secret police, the GPU. McGregor's report from the August 31 meeting notes that Hansen said "he was himself approached by an agent of the GPU and asked to desert the Fourth International and join the Third." The report states that Hansen met with a GPU handler named "John" for three months.[38] Hansen's astonishing admission brought heightened attention to these meetings.

Several days later, on September 4, Hansen returned to the US Embassy and provided the government with a "memorandum of conversation." A second report from George P. Shaw to the US Secretary of State was labeled "Strictly Confidential" and dated September 4. It reads: "I have the honor ... to enclose as of particular interest to the Department a copy of a memorandum

---

36. Letter from George P. Shaw to US Secretary of State Enclosing Memorandum of Conversation Between Robert G. McGregor and Hansen, September 1, 1940. (Cited in *The Gelfand Case: A Legal History of the Exposure of U.S. Government Agents in the Leadership of the Socialist Workers Party*. Vol. 1. Detroit, MI: Labor Publications, 1985, p. 7).

37. Ibid. (*The Gelfand Case*, p. 8).

38. Ibid.

of conversation handed in at this office by Mr. Joseph Hansen, secretary to the late Mr. Trotsky, on September 4, 1940."[39]

The September 4 report notes that "Mr. Hansen informed a member of my staff" regarding details behind the August 20 attack on Trotsky. A memorandum attached to the report notes that Hansen "said he would be very glad to have a copy [of unpublished writings by Trotsky] furnished to the Consulate General."[40]

On September 14, embassy official McGregor sent another "strictly confidential" letter to the State Department noting that Hansen had returned to the consulate that day to turn over confidential information to the US government. The report begins: "Mr. Joseph Hansen, Secretary to the late Leon Trotsky, called this morning and exhibited a memorandum, a photostat of which is attached."[41] This was the "W Memorandum"—a list of names of GPU agents the SWP had received from Whittaker Chambers, a former member of the Communist Party who later aided the US government in the anti-communist witch-hunt of the late 1940s and early 1950s.

The September 14 report also notes that Hansen provided the government with information regarding Albert Goldman. The report notes: "Hansen said that Albert Goldman, lawyer for the late Leon Trotsky, questioned Jacson yesterday ["Jacson" was an alias of Ramon Mercader, Trotsky's assassin]. Jacson told him that he had forwarded a suitcase on June 13, 1940 in bond via Railway Express to the Customshouse in New York in his own name..."[42]

On September 25, 1940, another letter from the US Embassy in Mexico to the State Department informed Washington that "Mr. Joseph Hansen, Secretary to the late Mr. Trotsky, called at this office yesterday..." Hansen then provided information which he obtained as a result of "questioning" individuals connected to Ramon Mercader, including Sylvia Ageloff, a young SWP member whom Mercader had seduced in an attempt to gain access to Trotsky's home in Coyoacan.[43]

Another letter dated September 25, sent by George P. Shaw to Raymond E. Murphy of the US State Department, includes the following passages: "I

39. Letter from George P. Shaw to US Secretary of State Enclosing Memorandum for File of Robert G. McGregor, September 4, 1940 (*The Gelfand Case*, p. 10).

40. Ibid., pp. 10, 11.

41. Memorandum of Robert G. McGregor of Conversation with Joseph Hansen, September 14, 1940 (*The Gelfand Case*, p. 13).

42. Ibid. (*The Gelfand Case*, p. 14).

43. Letter from George P. Shaw to US Secretary of State, September 25, 1940 (*The Gelfand Case*, p. 19).

am resorting again to a personal letter in order to acquaint you with a desire of Mr. Joseph Hansen, secretary to the late Mr. Trotsky, to establish confidential means by which he may be able to communicate with you and through you to this office from New York City."[44]

George P. Shaw further notes that Hansen "believes it possible that certain information may become available to him in which the Department will be interested ... For this reason he wishes to be put in touch with someone in your confidence located in New York to whom confidential information could be imparted with impunity."[45]

In response to Shaw's letter conveying Hansen's request to impart "confidential information" in return for "impunity," Raymond E. Murphy phoned J.B. Little of the FBI on September 28. In a follow-up letter dated that same day, Murphy wrote to his FBI contact: "It is further understood that Hansen is desirous of ascertaining the name of some person with whom he may communicate in the event he develops any information. Consequently, it would be appreciated if your New York office would send an agent to interview him in about ten days by which time he should be located in New York."[46]

Also on September 28, Raymond Murphy of the State Department wrote to George P. Shaw of the US Embassy "regarding the desire of Mr. Joseph Hansen to establish means by which he may communicate with me and through me to your office ... I would suggest that Mr. Hansen be informed that he get in touch with Mr. B.E. Sackett, Room 607, United States Court House, Foley Square, New York City, and use that office as a liaison. Mr. Sackett, agent in charge of the New York District of the Federal Bureau of Investigation through its office in Washington, is developing the investigation of the Trotsky case in the United States. The Department much prefers that these channels be employed as, strictly speaking, it has no means of its own to go into the extensive investigation needed for a case of this character ... The Federal Bureau of Investigation has been apprised of Mr. Hansen's departure and will undoubtedly contact him in New York."[47]

---

44. Letter from George P. Shaw to Raymond Murphy, US State Department, September 25, 1940 (*The Gelfand Case*, p. 21).

45. Ibid.

46. Letter from Raymond E. Murphy to Mr. J.B. Little, Federal Bureau of Investigation, September 28, 1940 (*The Gelfand Case*, p. 23).

47. Letter from Raymond E. Murphy to George P. Shaw, September 28, 1940 (*The Gelfand Case*, pp. 24–25).

On September 30, George P. Shaw wrote to Hansen "[in] answer to the inquiry you made here [in Mexico City] prior to leaving for the United States." Shaw informed Hansen that B.E. Sackett was to be his "intermediary." In a handwritten note, McGregor said: "Dear Joe: Please acknowledge receipt of this and indicate condition received in," so as to ensure that nobody, SWP member or otherwise, had opened the letter addressed to "Dear Joe."[48]

News that Hansen sought to "impart confidential information" with "impunity" soon made its way to J. Edgar Hoover, who became personally involved in overseeing the government's meetings with Hansen and the management of his status as an informant.

In an October 1, 1940 letter to B.E. Sackett, J. Edgar Hoover acknowledged that "Joseph Hansen, Secretary to the late Leon Trotsky, is leaving Mexico City shortly for New York City where he intends to conduct some independent investigation into the assassination of Trotsky. He has requested advice from the State Department as to whom he can contact to furnish any information that he may develop. ..."[49]

Hoover ordered the FBI to accept Hansen's offer to impart information with impunity: "Should Hansen call at the New York Office, he should be handled tactfully and all information which he can supply and his assistance in this investigation should be obtained. No information, of course, should be furnished him concerning the progress of the investigation by the Bureau."[50]

On October 23, Hansen replied to George P. Shaw's September 30 letter: "I received your letter concerning Mr. Sackett in good condition and shall visit him shortly."[51] Hansen was notifying the government that no members of the SWP had intercepted the letter.

The SWP leadership's testimony regarding Hansen's communications

Hansen carried out his meetings with the US government behind the backs of the leadership of the SWP. Several leading figures of the SWP denied having any knowledge of Hansen's communications with the government

48. Letter from George P. Shaw to Joseph Hansen, September 30, 1940 (*The Gelfand Case*, p. 26).
49. Letter from J. Edgar Hoover to B.E. Sackett, Special Agent in Charge, October 1, 1949 (*The Gelfand Case*, p. 29).
50. Ibid. (*The Gelfand Case*, p. 29–30).
51. Letter from Joseph Hansen to George P. Shaw, October 23, 1949 (*The Gelfand Case*, p. 31).

and insisted that the leadership did not consider approaching the FBI after Trotsky's death.

On June 2, 1977, David North, the national secretary of the Workers League, the predecessor of the Socialist Equality Party, interviewed Felix Morrow, a Smith Act defendant who served on the SWP Political Committee in 1940.

> Q: I was wondering whether or not you had any recollection about the steps taken by the Socialist Workers Party at the time to learn more about the assassination, how it was carried out. Particularly whether it received any assistance from the American government in any way.
>
> Morrow: None.
>
> Q: None whatsoever?
>
> Morrow: None.
>
> Q: Well, what was the attitude of the FBI, in your opinion, toward the assassination?
>
> Morrow: They weren't involved in any way.
>
> Q: Well, did the SWP to your knowledge have any policy of trying to obtain the assistance of the FBI?
>
> Morrow: There would be no reason. It was an open and shut case. Jacson had done it. The only problem was to establish that Jacson was a GPU agent.
>
> Q: I see. Then to your knowledge the SWP made no initiative at any time toward establishing contact with the FBI?
>
> Morrow: None. None.
>
> Q: Nothing at all?
>
> Morrow: I'm sure of that.
>
> Q: You're sure of that?
>
> Morrow: Yes.
>
> Q: Let me ask you something. Who was more or less in charge in the party with investigating the death of Trotsky? I know that Goldman wrote a book on the assassination.
>
> Morrow: Well, all involved—you know, the whole Pol-Com (Political Committee).
>
> Q: I see. How about Joseph Hansen?
>
> Morrow: He was down in Mexico.
>
> Q: And when he came back in late September 1940?

Morrow: He was not a member of the Pol-Com.

Q: And therefore he would not have been given a special responsibility?

Morrow: No.

Q: Does the name Sackett mean anything to you?

Morrow: No.

Q: It means nothing to you?

Morrow: Nothing.

Q: Politically speaking, in that period of time, as I recall there was some serious problem in terms of repression against the SWP and the labor movement by the FBI. This was before the war.

Morrow: Uh-huh.

Q: In 1940, around the period of August, had the repression already started, building up toward the Minneapolis case?

Morrow: I would say so.

Q: In what particular way?

Morrow: I couldn't really remember the details, but you know…

Q: The heat was on?

Morrow: Yes, the heat was on.

Q: And by the beginning of 1941, it probably became quite serious?

Morrow: Yes.

Q: In light of that, how would the party have looked upon an attitude—given Trotsky's political positions on defense of the workers' state, his attitude toward imperialism and Stalin— how would the SWP leadership at that point, the Political Committee, have looked upon reliance on the FBI in terms of—

Morrow: There was no reliance on the FBI.

Q: I see.

Morrow: It just didn't exist.

Q: But politically speaking, it would have been considered out of the ordinary…

Morrow: Of course!

Q: … for someone to suggest that be done?

Morrow: Yes.

Q: I'm asking this because the question has come up in documentation, but to you that would be complete news.

Farrell Dobbs, James P. Cannon and Felix Morrow

Morrow: That's right.

Q: I see, and you're quite sure that there was never any authorization.

Morrow: None.[52]

Morrow's statements were supported by the depositions taken of SWP Political Committee members Farrell Dobbs and Morris Lewit, and of Morrow, during the Gelfand Case.[53] Each of these leading SWP officials testified that he had no knowledge of Hansen's secret meetings with the FBI.

---

52. Interview by David North of Felix Morrow, June 2, 1977.

53. The Gelfand Case was a civil lawsuit brought by Alan Gelfand, a member of the SWP who was expelled for raising questions about Hansen's communications with the FBI and GPU. Gelfand sued alleging that the US government was violating his First Amendment rights by using its agents in the SWP to expel him from a political organization.

On April 11, 1982, Dobbs was questioned by Gelfand's attorney, John Burton:

> Burton: Did you know that in 1940 Mr. Hansen had face-to-face meetings with the FBI in New York City?
> Dobbs: I did not...
> Q: Did you ever talk to Mr. Hansen about his meetings with the FBI?
> A: I told you I know nothing about it.[54]

Morris Lewit led the SWP while Cannon, Morrow, Dobbs and others were imprisoned. He was deposed on April 13, 1982 and gave similar testimony.

> Gelfand: At that time did you know whether or not Hansen had met with the FBI in New York City following Trotsky's assassination?
> Lewit: I might have known it from the Healyites' statements, the documents. I don't know.
> Q: Did you consider at that time that allegation to be a lie?
> A: Not a lie, but if—I knew if anything Joe did was done with the knowledge of the party leaders and under their direction. He was that type of person.[55]

Hansen did not inform the leadership of the SWP about his meetings with the FBI. A December 9, 1940 report by FBI Special Agent M.R. Griffin details the agent's visit to SWP headquarters:

> The writer interviewed James P. Cannon and Joseph Hansen regarding the Trotsky affair and was advised by them that they had no information to offer. They appeared very reluctant to discuss the matter and gave very brief answers to questions put to them by reporting agent.[56]

---

54. Deposition of Farrell Dobbs, *Gelfand v. Smith et al.*, pp. 178, 182.
55. Deposition of Morris Lewit, *Gelfand v. Smith et al.*, p. 144.
56. Report by Special Agent M.R. Griffin, December 9, 1940, 62-6870, p. 8. (See Appendix B, p. 147).

The internal US government reports indicate that Hansen evinced no "reluctance" to talk to government officials in private. It was only when confronted by the FBI in the presence of James P. Cannon that Hansen kept silent.

The timing of Hansen's meetings with the US government

In *Trotskyists on Trial*, Donna Haverty-Stacke lays out evidence that the FBI's infiltration of the SWP underwent a fundamental change in the autumn of 1940, at precisely the time Hansen established contact with the FBI. FBI Agent Roy T. Noonan testified at trial that the agency developed specific files on key SWP leaders "*in the latter part of 1940.*"[57] (Emphasis added).

Haverty-Stacke notes that this infiltration was intensified in the spring of 1941, at which time the SWP's New York headquarters was "riddled with well-placed informants."[58] "The FBI watched the SWP's national headquarters in New York in particular very closely."[59]

Hansen wrote to George P. Shaw on October 23, 1940 that he "shall visit him [FBI Agent B.E. Sackett] shortly" at his office in New York. Hansen had requested the meeting earlier for the express purpose of imparting "confidential information" with "impunity" to the government.

Hansen returned to New York City in the "latter part of 1940," and Agent Noonan placed emphasis on "November 1940" as the date the infiltration reached a higher stage. Such a date strongly correlates with Hansen's return to the US and the fact that he promised *on October 23* that he would visit with B.E. Sackett *shortly*, i.e., at the end of October or early November 1940.

The public record of the communications between Hansen and the FBI stops after the October 23, 1940 note. This indicates that after Hansen returned to New York, the relationship took on a higher level of confidentiality and was subject to more stringent classification rules, which have hidden the communications from public view.

Joseph Hansen's request for "impunity"

Haverty-Stacke's book provides a context for the peculiar language included in the agreement Hansen sought, in which he would receive

57. Haverty-Stacke, p. 100 (Citing cross examination of Agent Roy T. Noonan, *US v. Dunne et al.*, p. 372).

58. Ibid., p. 155.

59. Ibid., p. 154.

"impunity" in return for sharing information with the government. According to *Black's Law Dictionary*, "impunity" means: "Exemption from punishment; immunity from the detrimental effects of one's actions. Cf. Immunity."[60] Hansen's request for personal legal protection had a purely individual character. He would not have made such a request if he had been contacting the FBI with the approval of the SWP.

There are two likely reasons why Hansen would have sought exemption from punishment by the government.

The first related to the disappearance of George Mink. J. Edgar Hoover stated specifically that Hansen was to be questioned concerning the disappearance of Mink, a Stalinist agent who vanished in the early part of 1940 and was presumed murdered. Hansen's admitted ties to the GPU gave the FBI reason to believe he was linked to Mink's disappearance.

In his October 1, 1940 letter to B.E. Sackett, J. Edgar Hoover provided his agent with background information surrounding Hansen's ties to the GPU and his possible knowledge of Mink's disappearance.

Hoover wrote:

> ...information has further been supplied by the State Department to the effect that Hansen and his associates liquidated George Mink six months ago, shortly before the first attack on Trotsky in May of 1940, by tying Mink up and throwing him into a crater some thirty miles from Mexico City...
>
> ...he should be handled tactfully and all information which he can supply and his assistance in this investigation should be obtained. No information, of course, should be furnished him concerning the progress of the investigation by the Bureau. However, every attempt should be made to determine the truth of the report concerning George Mink.[61]

The FBI was interested in Mink because he was a well known GPU agent and a US citizen. Mink, a former Philadelphia taxi driver, had traveled back and forth to Moscow and throughout Europe, where he was imprisoned in Denmark in 1935 as a Stalinist spy. Upon his release, Mink worked for the

---

60. *Black's Law Dictionary* (9th ed.) p. 826.
61. Letter from J. Edgar Hoover to B.E. Sackett, Special Agent in Charge, October 1, 1940 (*The Gelfand Case*, pp. 29–30).

GPU in Spain during the Civil War. The anarchist Carlo Tresca accused Mink of murdering the anarchist professor Camillo Berneri on behalf of the GPU in Barcelona.[62] His whereabouts and disappearance were of high importance to the FBI.

There is nothing to suggest that Hoover thought the Trotskyists were responsible for Mink's death. Hoover's use of the term "Hansen and his associates" is a reference to the GPU, which Hoover suspected of killing Mink. As a matter of political principle, the Trotskyists did not engage in assassination of opponents, and could not have been responsible. Moreover, they had neither the manpower nor the skill to carry out the assassination of a skilled GPU killer. The breach of Trotsky's residence in Coyoacan by the Stalinist assassination team in May 1940 and the failure of the guards to return fire give an indication of the inexperienced character of Trotsky's defense guard.

A second reason for Hansen to seek exemption from punishment stemmed from the possibility that the government would prosecute the SWP. Hansen used Trotsky's assassination as a pretext to establish ties with the government. At this point, the FBI was already active in monitoring the SWP and was considering the possibility of prosecution. By requesting legal "impunity," Hansen sought to ensure that neither his past actions nor the information he provided would be used against him as grounds for indictment or prosecution. The fact that he did not appear as a defendant or even as a witness in the trial indicates that he did, in fact, receive impunity.

Joseph Hansen's absence from the Smith Act trial

The prosecution's theory of the case was based on showing a connection between the chief conspirator, Leon Trotsky, and the Socialist Workers Party. This required a detailed showing of each and every connection between Trotsky, who was living in exile in Mexico City, and the Socialist Workers Party.

The prosecution brought forward the entire weight of evidence collected after months of investigation involving hundreds of witnesses and countless undercover agents to establish the connection between Trotsky in Mexico City and the SWP defendants. Beyond the hundreds of pages of documents

---

62. Dewar, Hugo, "Chapter 7: The Lady Vanishes." *Assassins at Large, Being a Fully Documented and Hitherto Unpublished Account of the Executions Outside Russia Ordered by the GPU*, (Boston: Beacon, 1952).

showing the SWP's political support for Trotsky's program, the evidence included:

- A March 1939 photograph showing James Bartlett, defendant Harry DeBoer and their wives posing with Trotsky in Mexico
- Testimony that defendant Emil Hansen had traveled to Mexico City to receive advice from Trotsky about establishing union defense guards
- Testimony that defendants Vincent R. Dunne and James Cannon had visited Trotsky in early 1939, along with Max Shachtman, also for the purpose of discussing union defense guards
- Testimony that defendant Jake Cooper served as a guard for Trotsky in Coyoacan
- Evidence that defendant Carl Skoglund drove to Texas in early 1938 with a group of SWP leaders who then visited Trotsky
- Records from a Texas auto body shop showing that a Pontiac car owned by the Minneapolis Teamsters local, and driven by Vincent R. Dunne, broke down in January 1938 en route to Mexico from Minneapolis
- Testimony that defendant Farrell Dobbs told Minneapolis SWP members in early 1938 that guards were needed to defend Trotsky in Mexico City
- Testimony that Dobbs himself visited Trotsky in Mexico City
- A photograph of Trotsky from August 1, 1938, signed by Trotsky and addressed to Vincent R. Dunne
- Testimony that defendant Albert Russell had a photograph of Trotsky in his work office
- A reference in Cannon's memorial address after Trotsky's assassination in which he notes visiting Mexico to help strengthen Trotsky's guard

One name emerges as an obvious evidentiary keystone to the prosecution's case: Joseph Hansen. Hansen lived with Trotsky in the latter's compound in Coyoacan and served as his political secretary from 1937 until Trotsky's assassination. He participated in daily political discussions with Trotsky and was chiefly responsible for overseeing communication between the SWP and Coyoacan. Many of Trotsky's communications to the SWP dating from this period were signed "J. Hansen" for security purposes.

Hansen personified the connection between the SWP and Trotsky, the precise legal issue the prosecution sought to prove. He was intimately familiar with the discussions between the SWP leadership and Trotsky regarding the split with the Burnham-Shachtman faction of the SWP in 1939–40, the development of the party's policy toward conscription in World War Two, and the development of the policy for the establishment of union defense guards. Each of these issues, and, in particular, the latter two, were repeatedly used by the prosecution to show that the SWP and Trotsky were engaging in a conspiratorial plan to overthrow the US government.

The US attorneys were aware of Hansen's position as Trotsky's secretary and Hansen's name is referenced multiple times in the course of the trial. From a prosecutorial standpoint, the fact that Hansen was not even subpoenaed to testify defies explanation.

Had the SWP leadership known of Hansen's visits with the FBI, the SWP's defense attorneys would have made heavy use of this key fact at trial.

First, it would have been a major political embarrassment for the Roosevelt administration if it became known that it had held secret meetings with a group it was now prosecuting for conspiracy to overthrow the government.

Second, the fact that the FBI had infiltrated the SWP leadership in advance of the trial would have served as evidence of the anti-democratic, frame-up character of the trial. The defense attorneys could have moved for a mistrial on the grounds that the secret meetings made it impossible to differentiate between the genuine plans of the SWP and suggestions made by government agents and FBI officials. Proof of Hansen's meetings could have been used to show that the FBI sought to entrap the SWP into advancing conspiratorial demands, rendering the whole trial illegitimate.

Third, the SWP could have used the meetings to expose the FBI's infiltration network by calling government witnesses and asking them, under oath, about any agents and informants operating within the party. The SWP could have turned the trial into an exposure of state surveillance. The issue of government infiltration of the labor movement was a major one in the late 1930s and early 1940s. The question occupied thousands of pages of testimony before the subcommittee on civil liberties of the Senate Committee on Education and Labor. The subcommittee was led by Wisconsin Senator Robert LaFollette.[63]

The prosecution's definition of a conspirator

In the course of his argument, US Attorney Anderson asserted defendant Goldman's guilt on the grounds that "he was a member of the Editorial Board

---

63. For further details, see *The Labor Spy Racket*, by Leo Huberman, U.S. Congress Senate Committee on Education and Labor, Modern Age Books, NY, NY, 1937.

of the Fourth International [Magazine], with James P. Cannon, with Felix Morrow, with Joe Hansen—Secretary for Leon Trotsky—and others..."[64]

Given that the prosecution claimed Goldman was implicated in the alleged conspiracy against the government by virtue of his serving on an editorial board with Hansen, "Secretary for Leon Trotsky," it follows legally that Hansen himself met the prosecution's definition of a conspirator. In addition, the prosecution introduced into evidence an article penned by Hansen and titled "Wall Street's War, Not Ours."[65] In other words, the prosecution felt that the writings of Hansen advanced the criminal conspiracy to overthrow the government. What's more, the prosecution referred to Hansen by the familiar name "Joe," despite the fact that he was listed as "Joseph Hansen" in the party press. Albert Goldman, James Cannon and Felix Morrow were not referred to as "Al," "Jim," or "Fritz," yet the government called Joseph Hansen "Joe."

In criminal law, those engaged in a conspiracy are responsible for all acts of the other conspirators in furtherance of that conspiracy, with one exception. As the prosecution noted in its argument at trial, a conspirator can absolve himself of complicity only by taking "some affirmative and effective act to disassociate himself from that criminal group."[66]

The most common form of such an "affirmative act" in American criminal law is to inform on other members of the conspiracy.

The post-war FBI infiltration of the SWP

Even with the SWP's main leadership in jail, the FBI remained concerned that the party was a significant revolutionary force. The infiltration that began with the preparation for the 1941 prosecution was greatly expanded. Based on the acquisition of new information in the autumn of 1940, the FBI began to lay the foundation for a network of informants that gave the government a clear view into the inner workings of the SWP and the Fourth International.

During the Second World War, Hoover believed the SWP remained a significant political force. His nervousness is exemplified by a letter he sent to Assistant Attorney General Wendell Berge in May 1943 in which he notes that the SWP picketed a showing of the pro-Stalinist propaganda film *Mission to Moscow*.

---

64. Testimony of James Bartlett, *US v. Dunne et al.*, p. 228.
65. Ibid.
66. Closing Argument of US Attorney Anderson, *US v. Dunne et al.*, 2457.

Federal Bureau of Investigation
United States Department of Justice
Washington, D. C.

MAY 6 1943

5

MEMORANDUM FOR ASSISTANT ATTORNEY GENERAL
WENDELL BERGE

RE: SOCIALIST WORKERS PARTY

Information has been received that on the evening of April 30, 1943, members of the subject organization picketed the opening of the film "Mission to Moscow" playing at the Hollywood Theater, Times Square, New York City.

In connection with this picket, six females carried placards containing such titles as "Stalin is the Real Defendant in the Moscow Trials," "Mission to Moscow - Stalin's Crimes Against Labor," and "The John Dewey Commission Hearing Branded Moscow Trials as Frame Ups." Other individuals distributed pamphlets reportedly setting forth a summary of the findings of the John Dewey Commission. This pamphlet also allegedly stated that the reason for the film was to do a diplomatic favor for Stalin and to whitewash his crimes in return for Stalin's support of the Allied powers. James P. Cannon, National Secretary of the Socialist Workers Party, and approximately twenty other members of the Party were present at the picketing but did not participate. Many of the pamphlets mentioned above were distributed to members of the Armed Forces.

Copies of the above-mentioned pamphlet are being obtained and will be made available to you at a future date.

The above is being submitted for your information and to keep you currently advised concerning the activities of the subject group.

Very truly yours,

John Edgar Hoover

J. Edgar Hoover to Assistant Attorney General Wendell Berge, May 1943

"Information has been received that on the evening of April 30, 1943, members of the subject organization [the SWP] picketed the opening of the film 'Mission to Moscow' playing at the Hollywood Theater, Times Square, New York City," the memo reads.

Hoover reports the exact wording of the SWP's slogans and cites a pamphlet distributed at the picket. "James P. Cannon, National Secretary of the Socialist Workers Party, and approximately twenty other members of the Party were present at the picketing but did not participate. Many of the pamphlets mentioned above were distributed to members of the Armed Forces."

Example of detailed FBI report on individual SWP members from the Chicago branch

In 1945, Hoover disobeyed a Justice Department order that no further investigations of the SWP be carried out. It appears that the sources gained in "November 1940" through the spring of 1941 stayed on as long-term assets of the FBI. Hoover successfully shielded his assets from being exposed at trial.

In July 1945, the FBI "went after the SWP with a vengeance," Haverty-Stacke explains. "[Hoover] continued to gather reports on the party from agents stationed around the country, who worked closely with well-placed informants."[67] In the late 1940s, Hoover "maintained the steady flow of memos to the attorney general highlighting the possible dangers and alleged criminal activity of the party and of individual members, like Cannon and

---

67. Haverty-Stacke, p. 204.

Example of informant reports on international sections of the Fourth International

Carlson, found in the agents' reports that he also forwarded to the Justice Department on a regular basis."[68]

The "well-placed informants" within the leadership of the SWP remained in their positions and were not exposed by giving testimony during the trial.

Informants in the SWP's New York City headquarters and elsewhere seemingly had access to all correspondence that passed through the headquarters and branch leaderships. FBI reports include detailed descriptions of every major party plenum and conference as well as the positions that were taken by individual comrades. Informants provided the government with a laundry list

---

68. Ibid.

United States Department of Justic
Federal Bureau of Investigation
Washington 25, D. C.

PERSONAL AND CONFIDENTIAL

June 12, 1948

MEMORANDUM FOR THE ATTORNEY GENERAL

RE: SOCIALIST WORKERS PARTY
      INTERNAL SECURITY - SWP

The Socialist Workers Party will hold its National
Convention at the Irving Plaza Hotel from July 1 through 5, 1948,
and it is believed possible to cover the various sessions of the
Convention by technical means.

As you know, the Socialist Workers Party is a militant
Trotskyite group and as dangerous if not more so to the internal
security than the Communist Party. At the present time an extensive investigation is being conducted of the Socialist Workers
Party and the coverage of this National Convention is believed
desirable.

It is requested, therefore, that you authorize the use
of technical equipment in connection with our surveillance work
of the National Convention of the Socialist Workers Party at the
Irving Plaza Hotel, New York City, from July 1 through 5, 1948.

Respectfully,

John Edgar Hoover
Director

FILED
BY
ON JAN 30 956

Orig. appvd. as above and ret. to FBI 6-15-48   146-1-10

DEPARTMENT OF JUSTICE
JAN 12 1956
RECORD BRANCH

CONFIDENTIAL

June 12, 1948 Letter from J. Edgar Hoover requesting the 1948 SWP National Convention be bugged

of the work of Trotskyists internationally, including in the Eastern bloc and
in countries run by military dictatorships.[69]

Reports composed by agents in 1946–48 on branches of the SWP in
the US were sometimes sixty to eighty pages long. These reports included

---

69. *See* Boxes 109 and 110, SWP 146-1-10, including, for example, FBI Report 100-4013,
New York.

detailed, multi-paragraph reports on individual party members, their home addresses, the ages of their children, their places of employment, their places of birth, their citizenship status and details regarding personal relationships and affairs.

Throughout this period, FBI agents prepared detailed reports on the activities of key members. There were long reports regarding Cannon, Vincent Dunne, Grace Carlson and Farrell Dobbs—just some of those who remained subject to close monitoring after their release from prison.

The degree to which the FBI was able to intensify its infiltration of the SWP is exemplified by a June 12, 1948 letter from J. Edgar Hoover to the attorney general. Hoover writes: "At the present time an extensive investigation is being conducted of the Socialist Workers Party and the coverage of this National Convention is believed desirable. It is requested, therefore, that you authorize the use of technical equipment in connection with our surveillance work of the National Convention of the Socialist Workers Party at the Irving Plaza Hotel, New York City, from July 1 through 5, 1948."[70]

The structure of the FBI's post-war infiltration was as follows: The highest-level information came from at least twenty "Confidential Informants" who were in personal communication with FBI officials on a regular basis. FBI records indicate that these informants provided information about political meetings, disagreements and the state of the movement internationally. Certain agents, code-named "T-1" through "T-4," "T-14," "T-19" and "ND 452," had intimate knowledge of the leadership of all branches and clearly occupied key roles in the SWP leadership.

So valuable were a certain number of these agents that the FBI notes they were "not in a position to testify" in case the government decided to bring further prosecution. The fact that the FBI received full reports of political committee meetings and party plenums from different confidential informant sources shows that the highest levels of leadership were compromised by agents of the state.

A rung below the confidential informants was a network of lower-level sources and agents who were members of the SWP in local areas and reported to their specified handlers on local party activities, political disagreements, and the lives of individual members. The FBI had a ring of agents in place in all areas where the party had a presence.

---

70. June 12, 1948 Memorandum For the Attorney General, RE: Socialist Workers Party—Internal Security—SWP, Box 110 SWP 146-1-10.

C – S P Political Committee Meeting of August 5, 1947

     Confidential Informant ¹-14, a highly confidential source, not
in a position to testify, furnished temporarily a copy of a document entitled:
"DISCUSSIONS ON WORLD CONGRESS – PC MEETING, August 5, 1947". This document
which is believed to be a discussion at a political committee meeting of
the SWP reflected that MORRIS LEWITT, under his alias of STEIN, led the
discussion at this meeting, pointing out that the World Congress is the
most important gathering of the Fourth International to date and that in
STEIN's opinion it even exceeds the founding conference in importance.

Report from "Confidential Informant T-14, a highly confidential source, not in a position to testify" regarding SWP Political Committee meetings

Haverty-Stacke notes that the infiltration of the SWP during 1938–41 laid the foundation for a decades-long infiltration program. Hoover's requests for surveillance were granted by the Justice Department "through 1948 and beyond." Further, "As the Cold War heated up, Hoover's pursuit of the SWP took on added intensity. The investigation of the party expanded with the growth of anti-communist sentiment and the new mechanisms created to facilitate such sentiment during the early 1950s that became hallmarks of the Second Red Scare."[71]

Haverty-Stacke makes reference to the Socialist Workers Party's 1973 lawsuit against the FBI's launching of COINTELPRO operations against the SWP in 1961. She notes that the FBI used 1,300 agents against the SWP between 1961 and 1976, stealing over twenty thousand SWP documents and conducting over two hundred illegal break-ins. In 1986, a federal judge ruled that the FBI was "guilty of violations of the constitutional rights of the SWP ... and of [its] members," and granted the SWP a judgment of $264,000.[72] Haverty-Stacke writes that "with access to the FBI's files, he [District Court Judge Thomas Griesa] substantiated the SWP's contention that the bureau's investigations of its activities and members began in 1940."[73]

Yet even as the SWP's lawsuit dragged on, the party expelled one of its own members, Alan Gelfand, because he asked the SWP to explain the communications between Hansen and the FBI in 1940. The SWP denounced Gelfand, called the *Security and the Fourth International* investigation a "big lie," and collaborated with the government to protect known agents of the GPU from testifying as to the Stalinists' role in infiltrating the SWP. Hansen himself died in the weeks before the Gelfand Case began.

---

71. Haverty-Stacke, p. 204.
72. Ibid., p. 220.
73. Ibid.

There is an overwhelming body of circumstantial and direct evidence pointing to the role of Joseph Hansen as a government informant. During the Gelfand trial, Gelfand's lawyer, John Burton, gave the following description of the evidence against Hansen:

> The proof depends on an intricate web of circumstantial evidence which leads inexorably to the nexus between the infiltration of the SWP by agents of the federal government and the expulsion of plaintiff. The facts of this case are embedded in great historical events. Their ever-widening spiral sweeps back into the past, embracing within its bounds an increasing number of individuals, including Trotsky himself and those closest to him during his last heroic exile. If a more direct and less arduous road to truth were available, plaintiff gladly would have taken it. Nonetheless, when fact is added to fact, and each is evaluated in its proper relationship to the other, the conclusion becomes inescapable that something is very, very wrong with the leadership of the Socialist Workers Party.[74]

While documentary records exist proving the *beginning* of Hansen's confidential relationship with the FBI, no documents have yet surfaced showing that this relationship *ended*.

None of this evidence has been answered by Hansen's defenders.

---

74. *The Gelfand Case*, p. 175

An "Exemplary Comrade": The Socialist Workers Party's Forty-Year-Long Cover-up of Stalinist Spy Sylvia Callen

In May 1947 the Socialist Workers Party received information that Sylvia Callen, the personal secretary of long-time party leader James P. Cannon, was an agent of the Soviet secret police, the GPU. It quickly became clear that Callen had concealed critical personal information about her Stalinist background when she joined the SWP in 1938. For nearly nine years Callen had high-level and unrestricted access to the party's most sensitive information. However, rather than exposing Callen's murderous role as a spy within the Trotskyist movement, the Socialist Workers Party launched a cover-up that lasted nearly forty years. What follows is a historical account of the cover-up and its exposure by the International Committee of the Fourth International.

On Saturday, March 8, 1947, the Socialist Workers Party (SWP) ran a banner headline in its publication, the *Militant*, which read:

Stalin's guilt in Trotsky murder bared by ex-Daily Worker editor: Budenz discloses details of how 1940 assassination was

Published on the World Socialist Web Site August 14–17, 2018

prepared, implicates leaders of Communist Party in GPU conspiracy.[1]

The article detailed revelations from former American Stalinist leader Louis Budenz's forthcoming book *This Is My Story*. The SWP had acquired an advance copy and made its contents known for the first time.

The Militant said Budenz's book "now supplies conclusive evidence that top operators of Stalin's secret police worked for years on American soil to prepare the murder of Trotsky"

This Is My Story vindicated the Fourth International's insistence that the assassination of Trotsky had been ordered by Stalin and carried out by the GPU, the secret police of the Stalinist regime in the USSR.

The lead article on March 8 in the *Militant*, written by John G. Wright, explained, "As an eyewitness and direct participant, Budenz, who served the Kremlin loyally for ten years, now supplies conclusive evidence that top operators of Stalin's secret police worked for years on American soil to prepare for the murder of Trotsky."[2]

---

1. The *Militant*, March 8, 1947. Available at: https://www.marxists.org/history/etol/newspape/themilitant/1947/v11n10-mar-08-1947.pdf.

2. Ibid.

John G. Wright

Less than seven years had passed since a Stalinist agent, using the false name Frank Jacson, murdered Leon Trotsky in Coyoacan, Mexico City, and it was only a decade since the peak of the mass exterminations during the Great Terror of 1936–38 within the Soviet Union.

Aside from Trotsky's assassin, who eventually was identified as Ramon Mercader del Rio, while serving a twenty-year murder sentence in a Mexican prison, nobody had been punished or jailed for the crimes of the GPU. Budenz's book exposed the conspiracy behind Trotsky's murder. It not only confirmed that the assassination was ordered in Moscow. Budenz also named leaders and members of the American Communist Party (CPUSA) as accomplices.

Budenz revealed that in December 1936, a GPU agent asked to meet with him secretly in a nondescript restaurant on East Fourteenth Street.

"It was rather early in my Party career that I was summoned to meet members of the Soviet secret police working on American soil," he wrote.[3]

The agent, who spoke with a heavy Russian accent, described himself as "Richards." The two sat in a corner, the clatter of dishes from the dinner crowd in the background. "As we ate together, Richards quietly told me his purpose in seeing me. His

Cover of Budenz's book, This is My Story

commission was to investigate the condition of the Social Democrats, and to determine who among them and what Trotskyites and 'fascists' were making organized efforts to enter the Soviet Union."[4]

Just four months earlier, in August 1936, the first Moscow Show Trial had concluded, resulting in the execution of sixteen defendants, including Old

---

3. Budenz, Louis, *This Is My Story*, (New York: McGraw-Hill, 1947), p. 244.
4. Ibid., p. 245.

Bolsheviks Grigory Zinoviev and Lev Kamenev, for engaging in a "Trotskyite conspiracy." During the ensuing campaign of mass murder to terrorize and destroy opposition to the Stalinist regime, hundreds of thousands were executed or thrown into labor camps. The mere accusation of sympathy for Trotskyism meant a death sentence.

When the topic of discussion turned to the August trial, Budenz expressed his support. The GPU was now preparing purges on an international scale.

Louis Budenz in 1947

As the meeting between Budenz and "Richards" took place, Trotsky was aboard a tanker headed from Norway to Mexico, fleeing from a continent comprised of governments who had rejected his appeals for asylum. With Trotsky taking up residence in Mexico, the GPU was preparing its North American counterparts to carry out his assassination.

After this meeting, Budenz began his assignment:

> But where did I fit into an enterprise for the protection of the Soviet Union from plotters? I was readily told. I was to collect all the data I had on enemies of the Soviet Union within the Left or labor ranks, and specifically the Trotskyites. Their names were to be given and everything else about them that might be pertinent to this inquiry.[5]

The GPU knew it was the SWP—the leading section of the Fourth International—that was responsible for ensuring Trotsky's security in Mexico. As a result, Budenz wrote, "Particular attention was to be paid those who did much traveling, especially abroad."[6]

Budenz exposed CPUSA leaders Earl Browder and Jack Stachel as personally supervising the infiltration campaign. With their collaboration, Budenz was able "to move back and forth across Manhattan" meeting GPU agents and delivering information on the SWP.[7]

---

5. Ibid., p. 245.
6. Ibid., pp. 245–46.
7. Ibid., pp. 246.

In 1937, Budenz began working with an agent named "Roberts," a.k.a. Dr. Gregory Rabinowitz, a leader of the American Stalinist spy ring. Rabinowitz had been tasked with weaving a net of agents to entrap Trotsky, and Budenz was to help plot the most intimate details. Rabinowitz asked Budenz, "Can you tell me where the Trotskyites here get their mail from Trotsky in Mexico City?"[8] Budenz obliged, mining his sources for information and helping the GPU get to those close to Trotsky, always looking for information regarding the SWP's international correspondence.

Budenz wrote:

> Photographs, too, came into his [Roberts-Rabinowitz's] field of inquiry. He began to bring me a number, one after another, and ask, "Do you know this man? Or that?" For the most part they seemed to be men and women seeking Soviet visas. Then he inquired about certain names on lists, which he said were "Trotskyite couriers." One of these was an inconspicuous news-paperman working in and out of China, who later, I believe, became associated with Reuters. Another was Sylvia Ageloff, whose name became widely known as the woman who brought Leon Trotsky's assassin, "Frank Jacson," into Mexico.[9]

Mexican police hold the pickaxe that Mercader used to murder Trotsky in 1940

---

8. Ibid., p. 257.
9. Ibid., pp. 258.

Budenz and the GPU built a network of agents to acquire information about the Trotskyist movement and the SWP's communications with Trotsky. Rabinowitz would propose candidates and Budenz would supply information on them, providing the GPU with his appraisal of their political trustworthiness and abilities for espionage.

"Generally, he [Rabinowitz] asked me first about their Party records and then how they would fit into further underground work among the Trotskyites or other groups," Budenz wrote. "After getting the individual's record, my job was to size him or her up according to their attitudes and associations (if I knew them) in the past."[10]

The central purpose of the infiltration was to kill Trotsky. To this end, Budenz exposed how he helped put the GPU in touch with Ruby Weil, who orchestrated the meeting between her friend Sylvia Ageloff, a member of the SWP, and Mercader, Trotsky's future killer.

Rabinowitz asked Budenz "that I bring Miss Y [later identified as Ruby Weil], a young woman who he had learned was a friend of Sylvia Ageloff," to a meeting at a Chicago hotel.[11] Weil was later to work with Paris-based GPU agent Mark Zborowski, party name "Etienne," to give Mercader access to Trotsky's household in Mexico City through Ageloff. Zborowski was, at the time, a member of the Fourth International.

The rendezvous between Mercader and Ageloff took place in Paris in 1938. Beginning in 1939, the two traveled to Mexico City together, where Ageloff introduced Mercader, the man she knew as Frank Jacson, into Trotsky's household.[12] The Stalinist ring around Trotsky was growing tighter, and the stage for his death was being set.

SWP demands grand jury indict Stalinist spies and CPUSA leaders

In response to the Budenz revelations, the SWP immediately began to publish the new information as widely as possible, demanding an investigation into the Stalinists' role in infiltrating the Trotskyist movement and assassinating its founder and leader.

---

10. Ibid., p. 259.
11. Ibid.
12. Ibid., p. 262.

Ask Grand Jury To Investigate Trotsky Murder

Delegation Demands Probe of Stalin's Agents Who Plotted Assassination in New York City

NEW YORK, Mar. 17—District Attorney Frank J. Hogan was today urged to summon a special grand jury to investigate the conspiracy to murder Leon Trotsky, which was hatched in New York City by Stalin's secret police. A delegation headed by Socialist Party leader Norman Thomas, N. Y. City Councilman Louis P. Goldberg, and novelist James T. Farrell, held a 45 minute meeting with Jacob Grumet, assistant District Attorney, to demand action on the sensational revelations made by Louis F. Budenz in his recently published book, *This Is My Story*.

In his autobiography, the former *Daily Worker* editor and Communist Party national committee member, testifies from personal knowledge that GPU agents, aided by American Communist Party leaders, plotted their moves here which ended in the murder of Trotsky in Mexico City in 1940.

The delegation handed the District Attorney a statement signed by scores of prominent citizens, asking that "Earl Browder, Jack Stachel, Budenz himself, and all other Communist Party leaders, past or present, who are known to have been involved in the activities of the Soviet secret police in our community, or who are declared to have had knowledge of such activities should be subjected to judicial action as the facts may warrant."

The statement pointed out that "Budenz adds new and hitherto missing links to the chain of evidence presented during [the assassin] Jacson's trial in Mexico, which showed him to be a Soviet police agent." In his book, Budenz states that he himself was used by GPU agents to weave their web around Sylvia Ageloff, a trusted friend of Trotsky's household. The murderer, Jacson, used Sylvia Ageloff to gain access to the house and commit the crime.

"Terrorism from any quarter is incompatible with the free life of the labor and progressive movements and their democratic functioning," the statement read. "Such abhorrent methods must be exposed and fought without compromise to the very end."

During the interview, Thomas said that the assassination of Trotsky is not the only act of political murder on American soil in recent years which has been charged to the Russian secret police. He referred to the mysterious disappearance in 1937 of Juliet Stuart Poyntz, former Communist Party leader. In his book, Budenz discloses that he was told by "Comrade R," a national committee member of the Communist Party, (Continued on Page 2)

The Militant proclaimed that "the revelations of Budenz fill in the missing threads in the fabric of evidence that places the responsibility for the murder of Leon Trotsky on the shoulders of Joseph Stalin."

All this was reported in the pages of the *Militant*.[13] The front page article of March 8, 1947 explained: "Sinister and secret details connected with the assassination of Leon Trotsky by Stalin's hired killer in Mexico City in August 1940 have been disclosed by Louis F. Budenz."[14]

The *Militant* said Budenz's book "now supplies conclusive evidence that top operators of Stalin's secret police worked for years on American soil to prepare the murder of Trotsky" and that "American Stalinists, including Budenz himself, helped pave the way for the assassin 'Frank Jacson' to worm his way into Trotsky's home."[15]

The *Militant* detailed how the book described Budenz meeting "with the GPU chieftain in charge of 'Anti-Trotskyist' activities," an agent known as "Richards." Budenz "was consulted on the selection of spies to penetrate the Trotskyist ranks" and "contacted GPU chieftains at least once a week. No piece of information was deemed too unimportant."[16]

The article continued: "Stalin's murder machine was particularly eager to collect every scrap of information concerning Trotskyists who travelled abroad. They were in search of some individual whom they could enmesh in Europe in their murder plot." Budenz's book showed how the Stalinists "had laid all the preliminary groundwork in the United States in 1937 for the assassination of Leon Trotsky in Mexico in 1940."[17]

---

13. The *Militant*, March 8, 1947. Available at: https://www.marxists.org/history/etol/news-pape/themilitant/1947/v11n10-mar-08-1947.pdf.
14. Ibid.
15. Ibid.
16. Ibid.
17. Ibid.

The *Militant* proclaimed, "The revelations of Budenz fill in the missing threads in the fabric of evidence that places the responsibility for the murder of Leon Trotsky on the shoulders of Joseph Stalin."[18]

Based on Budenz's account of GPU infiltration and the plot to kill Trotsky, the SWP launched a public campaign to expose the GPU and the role of the CPUSA. The SWP immediately put forward the demand that a grand jury subpoena key Stalinists so those responsible for orchestrating the infiltration of the Trotskyist movement would be forced to testify about the penetration of the Trotskyist movement, and called for the exposure of those agents remaining in the movement.

The revelations and demands for an investigation had an immense political impact among broader circles of the political left, which the SWP fought to mobilize in a commission to demand a grand jury to investigate the role of the GPU and the CPUSA in Trotsky's death.

On March 17, 1947, an SWP-led coalition that included Socialist Party leader Norman Thomas presented a petition to the district attorney in Manhattan demanding the convocation of a grand jury. The SWP mobilized a number of leading political and intellectual figures, including the author James T. Farrell and academics John Dewey and Sidney Hook, who reflected popular anger over the news of the Stalinist plot and gave the demand for a grand jury a broad popular appeal that the state could not ignore.

On March 22, The *Militant's* lead headline read, "Ask Grand Jury To Investigate Trotsky's Murder—Delegation Demands Probe Of Stalin's Agent Who Plotted Assassination In New York City."[19] The *Militant* reported the delegation

> ... held a 45 minute meeting with Jacob Grumet, assistant District Attorney, to demand action on the sensational revelations made by Louis F. Budenz in his recently published book, *This is My Story*. In his autobiography, the former *Daily Worker* editor and Communist Party national committee member, testifies from personal knowledge that GPU agents, aided by American Communist Party leaders, plotted their moves here which ended in the murder of Trotsky in Mexico City in 1940.

---

18. Ibid.

19. The *Militant*, March 22, 1947. Available at: https://www.marxists.org/history/etol/newspape/themilitant/1947/v11n12-mar-22-1947.pdf.

> The delegation handed the District Attorney a statement signed by scores of prominent citizens...[20]

The statement delivered to the assistant District Attorney on March 17, 1947 read, in part:

> Earl Browder, Jack Stachel, Budenz himself, and all other Communist Party leaders, past or present, who are known to have been involved in the activities of the Soviet secret police in our community, or who are declared to have had knowledge of such activities should be subjected to official examination and such judicial action as the facts may warrant.
> ...Budenz adds new and hitherto missing links to the chain of evidence presented during Jacson's trial in Mexico, which showed him to be a Soviet police agent.[21]

The *Militant* reported that Norman Thomas also asked the district attorney for an investigation into other murders believed to have been carried out in New York City by the Stalinists, including the 1937 disappearance of Juliet Stuart Poyntz, a prominent member of the Communist Party suspected of opposing the Stalinist terror, and anarchist leader Carlo Tresca, gunned down in 1943.

> "There are many others," Thomas added. "The so-called 'suicide' of [Soviet defector Walter] Krivitsky in Washington—a phony if there ever was one! There is the murder of [defector] Ignace Reiss in Switzerland; the series of murders of Trotsky's secretaries and members of his family. We think the situation is so grave that immediate action is imperative to halt these political murders."[22]

The significance of Budenz's revelations and the weight of his word as an accomplice compelled the District Attorney's office to acknowledge "that the Budenz book could 'provide many leads,'" the *Militant* wrote.[23]

---

20. Ibid.
21. Ibid.
22. Ibid.
23. Ibid.

The May 3, 1947 issue of the Militant featured an article by Trotsky's widow Natalia Sedova titled, "Stalin's guilt—Budenz Book Supplies Link in GPU Murder of Trotsky."

The SWP expanded its campaign with the publication on May 3, 1947 of an article by Trotsky's widow Natalia Sedova titled, "Stalin's guilt—Budenz book supplies link in GPU murder of Trotsky."[24]

Sedova wrote:

> Everything we said in connection with the violent death of L.D. Trotsky is today being wholly confirmed by the confessions of Louis Budenz, a former leader of the American "Communist" Stalinist Party, in his book *This Is My Story* published in March of this year. ...
>
> The confessions of Louis Budenz throw into the limelight the entire activity of the secret Stalinist "Apparatus," which has usurped power and which acts with bloody arbitrariness.

Sedova continued:

> The participation of the leaders of the "Communist" Party of the U.S. in the plot against Trotsky, attested to by Louis Budenz,

---

24. The *Militant*, May 3, 1947. Available at: https://www.marxists.org/history/etol/news-pape/themilitant/1947/v11n18-may-03-1947.pdf.

provides sufficient grounds for bringing before the court Budenz himself together with Browder and Stachel and to place them in the hands of the Mexican judicial authorities.[25]

Within weeks of publishing Budenz's revelations, the SWP campaign for a grand jury compelled the district attorney to call Budenz to testify. For the first time since Trotsky's assassination, the SWP had caused a person with intimate knowledge of how the GPU murdered Trotsky to appear under oath in an American courtroom. The opportunity to expose the Stalinists' crimes and shed light on their infiltration of the Trotskyist movement had never been closer.

But just as a real investigation appeared likely, an event occurred that led the SWP to abort its campaign, denounce Budenz as a liar and abandon further efforts to expose Stalinist agents inside the Trotskyist movement.

A visit from Max Shachtman and Albert Glotzer

It had been seven years since Max Shachtman and Albert Glotzer split from the SWP to found the Workers Party when the two walked in to National Secretary James P. Cannon's office at 116 University Place, New York, in May 1947. Despite their political differences with the SWP, both men had long histories in the Trotskyist movement, and they held a principled position toward sharing information related to questions of political security.

Shachtman and Glotzer brought shattering news. They told Cannon that they had received reliable information that implicated his personal secretary, Sylvia Callen, whose party name was Caldwell, as a GPU agent.

James P. Cannon, Martin Abern and Max Shachtman in New York, 1938

---

25. Ibid.

Shachtman and Glotzer affirmed that the source was reliable and had provided them with correct information in the past. The source informed Shachtman and Glotzer that the Stalinists had moved Callen from Chicago to New York in 1939 for the purposes of infiltrating Cannon's office. Their source said Sylvia had been in a relationship with a young Stalinist from a Stalinist family whose father was a doctor.

The 1947 Control Commission

Sylvia Callen/Franklin/Caldwell

Callen was, in the language of the day, Cannon's "Girl Friday." She handled all of his political and personal affairs. She organized Cannon's schedule, had access to all party records, finances and international correspondence, and took dictation of his letters, memoranda and political reports. If Callen were an agent, it meant the security of the SWP and the Fourth International had been severely compromised by the GPU. All important information that crossed Cannon's desk had been read by the GPU and transmitted to the Kremlin, including details of Trotsky's security in Coyoacan.

Alongside the evidence of Callen's role, Shachtman and Glotzer also informed Cannon that their source stated there was an FBI agent in the party leadership.

On May 26, 1947, Cannon convened a meeting of the Control Commission, the party organization responsible for internal investigations. The ICFI has accessed the minutes of the May 26, 1947 and subsequent commission meetings in the Hoover Institute at Stanford University, and publishes them here: (See Appendix B, pp. 158–163)

> Meeting of Control Commission, May 26, 1947.
> Report by Martin [Cannon]:
> For several years the WP [Workers Party] has been sending
> us reports that they have information which would indicate that

the FBI had an agent in our party, high in the leadership. They claimed that their source of information had proven correct in several instances and that they believed this source was reliable.

Recently Shachtman and Gould [Glotzer] talked with Cannon and told him that the same source had informed them as follows:

The Stalinists have a woman in the SWP and that her name is S.

She came from Chicago in 1939 and that she worked there in a doctor's office.

She has or had a boy friend whose name is Irving.

Gould insisted that she came from the YCL.

This information pointed to Comrade S.

MOTION: That the case be thoroughly investigated by the Control Commission.

That we have a session with S. to get her biographical story and then call in Shachtman and Gould.

Carried.

First meeting with S. set for Thurs. evening May 29, 1947.

Three days later, on May 29, Callen appeared before the Commission. The facts relating to her background largely substantiated the information provided by Shachtman and Glotzer. It was quickly established that Callen had concealed critical aspects of her personal and political background and associations, including the fact that she was married and that her husband, Zalmond Franklin, was a leading Stalinist from a prominent Communist Party family in Wisconsin.

The May 29 meeting minutes read as follows:

Case of Comrade S.

May 29, 1947.

In response to questions put to her by members of the Secretariat and Control Commission in combined session, the following biographical sketch was given:

My father's name is John Callen. He has been a salesman for many years. Neither he nor any other member of my family entertain or ever entertained any political views other than the average citizen.

I myself did not know that there was such a thing as a radical movement until I was about 19, at college.

I lived in Milwaukee until about 1932. I went to Madison, Wisc. to attend the University of Wisconsin. There I met Zalmond Franklin and we got married in February 1935. We were together on and off for about a year. I graduated June 1935 and left school. Franklin remained at school. After graduating I looked for work and finally found a job in a Milwaukee drug store and worked there for a while as sales clerk.

In the Fall of 1935 or Spring of 1936 I went to Chicago to live with my folks. There I entered the Chicago University to study social service. I went to school there for four quarters, working one summer for the Jewish Social Service outfit there, and then went to work for the Chicago Relief Administration where I worked until I came to New York.

In the summer of 1937 I joined a YPSL [Young Peoples' Socialist League—the youth movement of the Socialist Party, within which the SWP conducted its activity at the time] circle in Chicago.

I came to New York in May 1938 to go to work for the Hebrew Association for the Deaf. I worked part time there and helped out in the National Office of the SWP in spare time. In December 1939 [here there is a strike out over the "9" and a line to a margin correction which reads "1938"] I was asked to take a full-time job in the SWP National Office as the office secretary was leaving to take a job in industry.

On direct questioning of Cannon, the following answers were given:

My first contact with radicalism was at Wisconsin University where there was a group of the National Students' League. My husband joined the League, 1935 semester, and I joined too just because he did. But I really didn't know what it was all about. I don't know whether the YCL [Young Communist League—the youth movement of the Stalinist Communist Party] had a fraction there at the time, but there was a radical group, bohemian types, of which my husband was one, and which was considered the "Communists" on the campus. I never knew whether my husband had any communist affiliations, but knew he was radical in his views and he may have been a member. I do know that his parents were either communists in ideology or just on the fringe of the Communist Party. They once gave a house party for the Friends of the Soviet Union.

Some years ago I heard that my former husband had been in Spain during the revolutionary days there. So I imagine he must have become a YCLer after our separation. Or he may very likely have been one before. I did not know enough then to be able to detect that and he never trusted me with any information about his activities.

"Did you ever belong to the YCL?"

No, never. I knew of the existence of such an organization but reacted against it emotionally because of the Bohemian character of the people around my husband who were considered "communists." But I did not really understand what communism was.

"How did you come to join the YPSL? Any member of your family interested in Socialism?"

No, none of my family ever had or have now any radical views. I came to join the YPSL chiefly I guess, because I was so lonely. I did not fit in with the friends of my family and I had no circle of my own. At the University in Madison, I got my first contact with radicalism and in a vague way I got to feel that socialism is a good thing. I heard Norman Thomas speak at the Socialist Club of the University of Chicago and he made a deep impression on me. I wanted to know more about socialism, so in my loneliness, I consulted the Chicago telephone directory for the address of some socialist organization, and founf [sic] the Socialist Bookstore.

At the time, I was working as a social worker in Chicago. The work I was doing, by the way, did not help me any. The patronizing attitude toward the poor was very distasteful to me. Well, so I went to the Socialist Party bookstore for some of their literature. There I met Lydia Beidel. She told me about the Young People's Socialist League in my neighborhood and invited me to attend. I went. They met at Belle's house. There I met a number of people. They seemed so different from the people I had known and made me feel so at home that I returned to a number of meetings and then joined the Circle. They were different from the other type of radicals I had known at college and I liked them as people. In the summer of 1937 I joined the YPSL circle on the North Side, Chicago.

Paul Picquet was the organizer of this circle. Most of the members of this circle were already Trotskyists. I came under their influence.

Several months after the Founding Convention of the Socialist Workers Party. [sic] I joined the party. The branch I joined had in it Goldman, Belle, Helen Judd, Shirley S, Irving Bern and all the other Landaus.

When I left for New York I was transferred. Here I was attached to the Village branch which met at Luttinger's. In this branch was Rose Karsner, Frieda Moore, Billie Ramloff.

"Did you ever work for a doctor in Chicago or Milwaukee?"

No, never. The only doctor I knew in those days was my husband's father. But I never worked for any doctor.

"Did you ever have a boy friend by the name of Irving?"

I may have casually known some student by that name, though I don't recall any. But I never had any close friend by that name.

Callen admitted that she had been a member of the Stalinist-aligned National Student League and that her husband, Zalmond Franklin, fought as a Stalinist in the Spanish Civil War and came from a Stalinist family. Until then, after eight years working in the national office, the SWP leaders had not known that Callen was married, let alone to a Stalinist. This was also the first time the party learned of her involvement with the Stalinist National Student League. But the SWP was grasping at straws when it claimed that Shachtman and Glotzer's reference to Callen's boyfriend "Irving" undercut the source's assertions. Every other detail substantiated the source as well as Budenz's revelations. In 1950, Budenz's second book, *Men Without Faces*, used the name "Irving" to refer to Zalmond.

The facts which Callen now revealed left no doubt that she had lied about her close connections with the Communist Party. But Zalmond Franklin was not merely a rank-and-file CP member or an innocent YCLer. Information that was readily available when the Control Commission convened showed Callen's husband was a prominent public representative of the Communist Party and a member of a leading Stalinist family.

Samuel Franklin with his son Zalmond—the fact that Sylvia Franklin's husband was a Stalinist was covered up by the SWP Control Commission

Zalmond David Franklin (1909–1958), and his father, Samuel Nathan Franklin (1882–1958), both served in the Spanish Civil War. Samuel Franklin was a doctor who was elected County Coroner in Milwaukee in 1918 as a member of the Socialist Party. Long active in politics, Samuel Franklin led the Milwaukee Medical Bureau of the Stalinist-led North American Committee to Aid Spanish Democracy during the civil war.[26]

According to ship travel log records, the elder Franklin was in Spain with the Abraham Lincoln Brigade as a medical adviser from July 1937 to February 1938.[27] Callen herself admitted on May 29, 1947 that her husband's father was a doctor.

---

26. "Samuel Nathan Franklin," Abraham Lincoln Brigade Archive, available at: http://www.alba-valb.org/volunteers/samuel-n-franklin

27. Ibid.

Zalmond Franklin was the second oldest of Samuel Franklin's three children. A University of Wisconsin bacteriology student, he served as an agent of the GPU in Spain from July 1937 to March 1938. His passport lists a Chicago address.[28] An article titled "Zalmond Franklin, 'Somewhere in Spain'" in the October 11, 1937 edition of the *Wisconsin State Journal* makes reference to the young Stalinist:

Zalmond Franklin, 'Somewhere in Spain'

Zalmond Franklin, former University of Wisconsin student, is with his father, Dr. Samuel N. Franklin, Milwaukee, in an American base hospital, "somewhere in Spain." Zalmond quit his bacteriology studies here early this year to go to Spain, and was followed by his father, head of the Milwaukee medical bureau of the North American Committee to Aid Spanish Democracy.

The Wisconsin State Journal article reporting Zalmond Franklin's travels "Somewhere in Spain"

> Zalmond Franklin, former University of Wisconsin student, is with his father, Dr. Samuel N. Franklin, Milwaukee, in an American base hospital "somewhere in Spain." Zalmond quit his bacteriology studies here early this year to go to Spain, and was followed by his father, head of the Milwaukee medical bureau of the North American Committee to Aid Spanish Democracy.[29]

In an article published in the *Wisconsin Jewish Chronicle* on May 6, 1938, Zalmond Franklin was referred to as a well-known public speaker on behalf of the Stalinists and their crimes in Spain. The *Chronicle* article reads:

> Zalmond Franklin, graduate student of bacteriology, left the U. of Wis. last June to serve the cause of democracy in republican Spain. He was in charge of all laboratory work in the four American hospitals in Spain. He left Spain this February, arriving in New York a month ago.
>
> At present he is touring the [middle] west telling of the terrific struggle in Spain and of his own unusual experiences. He will speak at the Jewish Center, 1025 N. Milwaukee street, this Saturday, May 7, at 8 p.m.[30]

28. "Zalmond David Franklin," Abraham Lincoln Brigade Archive, available at: http://www.alba-valb.org/volunteers/zalmond-david-franklin

29. "Zalmond Franklin, 'Somewhere in Spain,'" October 11, 1937, *Wisconsin State Journal*, p. 2.

30. "Experiences in Spanish War to Be Recounted," May 6, 1938, *Wisconsin Jewish Chronicle*.

Experiences in Spanish War to Be Recounted

Zalmond Franklin, graduate student of bacteriology, left the U. of Wis. last June to serve the cause of democracy in republican Spain. He was in charge of all laboratory work in the four American hospitals in Spain. He left Spain this February, arriving in New York a month ago.

At present he is touring the . west telling of the terrific struggle in Spain and of his own unusual experiences. He will speak at the Jewish Center, 1025 N. Milwaukee street, this Saturday, May 7, at 8 p. m.

The Franklin collection of original posters from the Spanish Ministry of Propaganda will be shown. Some of these posters were featured in a na-

An article from the Wisconsin Jewish Chronicle announcing the talks of Zalmond Franklin—Sylvia Callen's husband—on his unusual experiences in Spain

When Callen admitted to hiding her marriage to this Stalinist, the SWP had enough information to know she was a spy. All the SWP had to do was investigate the Franklin family by picking up the telephone and calling the Milwaukee branch or by inquiring with Harry Milton, an SWP member who fought in Spain with the Workers Party of Marxist Unity (POUM) while the Franklins were also present. Readily available reports in the local newspapers would also have shown the Franklins' roles as high-profile Communist Party figures. Callen provided the SWP with information that left no doubt about who she really was.

But when the party Control Commission met for the last time a week later on June 5, 1947, it covered up the evidence of Callen's marriage to Zalmond Franklin. A stenographic report of the meeting, titled "Case of Comrade S.," is published in full:

Case of Comrade S.
June 5, 1947.
Joint meeting of Control Comm. and Secretariat.

PURPOSE of meeting: To hear a report from WP members about rumors concerning comrade S which came to their attention.

Report by Shachtman:
About one, two or three weeks after Budenz's book, THIS IS MY STORY came out, a reliable friend of ours came and told me that an FBI agent called on him to get some information. In the course of the conversation the FBI man told our friend Jones that the Stalinists have an agent in the SWP. He then asked if Jones knew a certain "S" in the SWP who came from Chicago in 1939, got a job in the office of the SWP and then became private secretary to Cannon. In Chicago she worked for a doctor. She had a Stalinist boy friend by the name of Irving.

The WP comrades were then told of "S"'s biographical sketch as it was given to us by her.

Comrade G of the WP then told of the first time he met "S" at a membership meeting in Chicago in the NW side, about 1937.

The WP members assured us they had not talked to anyone about the matter and would not do so. They agreed there was nothing in the information they had except the statement of an FBI man, but felt duty-bound to report the matter to us.

Cannon pointed out that the only facts upon which the FBI man based the conclusion that she is a Stalinist agent in the SWP were:

1 - That comrade S came to New York from Chicago in 1939.

2 - That she had worked for a doctor in Chicago

3 - That she got a job as stenographer in the office of the SWP and later became Cannon's private secretary.

4 - That she had or has a boy friend named Irving.

Discussion followed and the general consensus of opinion was that the above points did not constitute any facts upon which to base any credence in the rumor or further action.

After the WP members left the discussion was continued and the following motion was made and carried:

MOTION: That there is no basis for suspicion of comrade S in the statements of the FBI man and that we so notify comrade S.

That we make no mention of the case to anyone and ask the WP comrades not to speak of it either.

That we watch for evidence of any gossip about this matter and in the event that such gossip develops we act promptly according to the circumstances dictated by the new developments.

Rose Karsner
Control Commission

The SWP response was a dishonest cover-up. Shachtman and Glotzer had provided the Control Commission with clear and actionable facts. The publicly available information about the Franklin family's role as public advocates for Stalinism proved definitively that Sylvia Callen had lied about her ties to the Communist Party.

The SWP would have been entirely within its rights to demand a grand jury investigation into Callen's role just as it had demanded with Louis Budenz. On June 5, 1947, the *same day* of the second SWP Control Commission meeting, Budenz finally appeared before a grand jury in New York. The SWP leaders had been in regular contact with the Manhattan District Attorney to whom they had delivered petitions demanding a grand jury indictment. Now, the SWP had evidence that the GPU had infiltrated the party leadership with an agent who had access to high-level internal material. This was a major breakthrough in the case to expose GPU infiltration of the Trotskyist movement.

But the SWP did nothing to investigate Callen's role. The party should have expelled Callen for lying and concealing her background. The *Militant* should have made this information public, adding to the Budenz revelations and the hemorrhaging of information relating to the GPU's infiltration of the SWP and its role in orchestrating the assassination of Leon Trotsky. Instead, the SWP leadership let her go, and passed a motion "that we make no mention of the case to anyone and ask the WP comrades [Shachtman and Glotzer] not to speak of it either." The Control Commission resolved, "in the event that such gossip develops we act promptly according to the circumstances dictated by the new developments." Cannon's wife and Callen's good friend, Rose Karsner, was the sole signatory on the June 5 stenographic report.

By withholding this crucial information, the SWP was obstructing the very investigation it had demanded in the first place.

Budenz's exposure of Callen was, without question, a devastating political and personal blow to Cannon. He would have immediately recognized the political implications of Callen's treachery. The security of the SWP had been fatally compromised. Callen had access to the party's documents, records, and international correspondence. Cannon was confronted with a nightmare that was all too real. Nevertheless, Cannon and the Control Commission had an inescapable political obligation to get to the truth of the matter. Instead, acting in a manner for which there could be no justification, they decided to organize a cover-up of Callen's role as a Stalinist spy.

Callen left the movement immediately after the SWP Control Commission and moved out of New York. Her sudden disappearance was neither reported nor explained to the membership. Moreover, Budenz's appearance before the grand jury was barely noted in the *Militant*; the SWP soon dropped its coverage of the Budenz revelations altogether.

Budenz's *Men Without Faces* and the House Un-American Activities Committee

In 1950, Louis Budenz published a second book, *Men Without Faces*, which provided an even more detailed description of the agent who had infiltrated the national headquarters of the SWP.

Budenz wrote: "Just before I went out to Chicago, in 1937 to become editor of *Midwest Daily Record* I had been instructed by Roberts [Dr. Gregory Rabinowitz, the GPU spy leader] to find a comrade who was engaged in penetrating the Trotskyite organization there."[31]

Though employing the pseudonym "Helen" in place of the spy's real first name, Sylvia, Budenz's biographical sketch left no doubt that he was telling the story of the GPU's recruitment of Sylvia Callen and her successful infiltration into the SWP's national headquarters.

> From out of the ranks of the Chicago YCL there came a young couple whom we shall call Helen and Irving. ... [The two] were assigned to dangerous secret work. Helen, being quiet and inconspicuous, was assigned to penetrate the Trotskyite groups. Irving, who went to Spain as a member of the Abraham Lincoln Brigade, was used as a special agent, under Steve Nelson and the forbidding George Mink, to detect and eliminate "enemies of the party. ..."
>
> ...Helen had been instructed to move to New York, in order to penetrate the Trotskyites on a national scale. ... I was then in

---

31. Budenz, Louis, *Men Without Faces* (New York: Harper and Brothers, 1950), p. 124.

Chicago, and it was I who had arranged this transfer, on the orders of the Soviet secret police representative with whom I was working and who was known to me only as "Roberts."[32]

Budenz described his first meeting with Callen:

Our first conference was at [YCL Chicago leader Jack] Kling's house out on the West Side of Chicago. With curtains drawn so that no one could see who was there, we arranged the ways and means by which I could get in touch with her. She expressed an eagerness to work on a wider scale for the party among the Trotskyites and, before she knew what the mission involved, gladly volunteered her services.[33]

Budenz was impressed by Helen-Sylvia's "soft voice and conservative dress, which suited her position as a social worker, enhanced her skill as an underground agent." Budenz "arranged to meet her privately at different places in South Chicago, where much of her social work was done." He convinced her to move to New York "[w]hen I had satisfied myself about her loyalty and capability."[34]

Budenz explained that Rabinowitz provided Callen with "$300 in cash to cover her first-class fare to New York and her initial expenses there. He then told her how she was to proceed. She would have an apartment in mid-Manhattan; and arrangements had been made for her apparent employment by a woman doctor who was a trusted

SWP offices in New York at 116 University Place, taken in 1975

---

32. Ibid., pp. 123–24.
33. Ibid., p. 125.
34. Ibid.

party member. This would explain her regular income and also her irregular hours. She could then volunteer to do stenographic and other clerical work at the Trotskyite national headquarters on University Place and 13th Street."[35]

Certain conditions were set. "[I]t was to be an unbreakable rule that Irving was never, for any reason, to go to her apartment; nor were they ever to be seen together in public."[36] The Stalinists were aware of Zalmond Franklin's public profile and his family's widely-known role as leaders of the Communist Party in Milwaukee. They knew that if the SWP discovered Callen's husband's identity, her role as a GPU spy would be exposed. Callen observed this rule, and concealed her marriage from the SWP.

> The arrangements went through at top speed: Helen departed for New York, and Irving soon was located in the Bronx. And Helen so ingratiated herself with the leading Trotskyites that she became a close friend of James Cannon, American Trotskyite chief, and his wife Rose Karsner. ... She had the full run of the Trotskyite offices, became Cannon's secretary, and made available to the Soviet secret police all the correspondence with Trotsky in Mexico City and with other Trotskyites throughout the world.[37]

Callen dictates the SWP's response to *Men Without Faces*

Budenz's account of Callen's activity in *Men Without Faces* was detailed and irrefutable. Nevertheless, the SWP leaders sought to maintain the public pretense that Callen had been a devoted and hardworking comrade.

But the pressure to come up with a response to Budenz was overwhelming. In August 1950, the Party leaders dispatched Farrell Dobbs to meet Callen at her home in Chicago to ask *her* how the party should reply.

Farrell Dobbs

---

35. Ibid.
36. Ibid., p. 126.
37. Ibid.

In an August 21 letter to Cannon, Dobbs reported on his meeting with Callen. He wrote:

Chicago, Ill.
August 21, 1950

Dear Jim,

I have seen S. When I showed her the passage in the Budenz book and told her of the Shachtmanite prattle she reacted with mingled anger against her detractors and anxiety for her family.

She told me the FBI has been hounding her and her family. As a result her father almost lost his job and was told that if there is any more investigating he will be fired. The FBI tried to question her about the party but she refused to give them any information.

Her family now knows the whole score and they have put heavy pressure on her to keep her away from the movement.

She does not want to be involved either directly or indirectly in the matter of a reply to Budenz. I asked if she would be willing to sit down with Mike and me to help us gather some of the facts needed to refute Budenz which would be used without openly or directly involving her. She said she did not want to be drawn into the thing in any manner whatever.

I told her that we considered it absolutely necessary to reply to Budenz charges. She asked if we couldn't just issue a statement announcing that a full investigation of his allegations was made three years ago which proved his story false and denounce him as a character assassin. She asked if the statement couldn't be general, i.e., not refer to any specific person in refuting him, but state that no such person as he describes has ever been in the party office.

She appeared to be in good health, seemed pleased to see me, and asked about everyone. She had not heard about Oscar [Coover, a longtime leader of the SWP who died earlier that year.]

So far as I can see there is no point in attempting to press her any further on this matter. It seems best to go ahead along the lines we agreed on when we discussed the question in the secretariat right after the last plenum.

(signed) Farrell (See Appendix B, p. 164)

The SWP sent Dobbs to meet Callen because they wanted to know whether she had spoken to the FBI about the party and its leadership. The bizarre, Dostoevskyan quality of the letter is a product of the fact that the SWP was going along with a story they had created which they knew to be a lie. By preventing any investigation into Callen's ties to the Communist Party and by calling Budenz's revelations and Shachtman and Glotzer's warnings "rumors" and "gossip," they created a false narrative that they felt they had to maintain.

Callen brazenly told the SWP how they should respond to Budenz's revelations. She instructed Dobbs to simply deny the existence of anyone who fit "Helen's" description, and to cite the 1947 Control Commission as proof that the allegations against her were baseless. The SWP leaders, in a decision that was as cowardly as it was duplicitous, acceded to Callen's instructions.

One week after Dobbs' letter, on August 28, 1950, Cannon published an article in the *Militant* acknowledging that the party had received a report of a possible GPU agent in the national headquarters. Calling Budenz a "well-known professional perjurer," Cannon wrote that the references to "Helen" in *Men Without Faces* were false:

> This story, published by Budenz for the first time in the middle of the year 1950, has been known to us for more than three years. In 1947, we received a "tip," purportedly emanating in the first instance from circles close to the FBI, that one of the secretarial workers in the National Office, who was identified by name and specifically by previous occupation and biographical details, was an agent of the Stalinists.[38]

Mischaracterizing Callen's role as a mere "secretarial worker" and not as his personal secretary, Cannon claimed that "[t]his report was promptly handed over to the party Control Commission for investigation according to the established principles of the revolutionary workers' movement" and that the investigation "established that the 'information' given to identify the accused comrade as to her biography, her previous occupation, and her personal life, was false. It was evident to us then that the accusation was based

---

38. The *Militant*, August 28, 1950, available at https://www.marxists.org/history/etol/news-pape/themilitant/1950/v14n35-aug-28-1950-mil.pdf

either on mistaken identity, or was a deliberately planted story designed to create a spy-scare in the organization."[39]

This account was a lie from beginning to end. The Control Commission covered up the fact that the testimony corroborated the report from Shachtman and Glotzer's source and that she lied about being married to a leading Stalinist. It concluded by swearing those present to secrecy and was signed by the accused's close personal friend, Rose Karsner. Far from proving the source's information was false, the Control Commission hearings confirmed she had moved to Chicago in 1939 and uncovered that she had not told the party she had been married to a Stalinist and had been in the Stalinist youth movement. She left the SWP as soon as her cover was blown. Under the circumstances there was no innocent explanation.

Following Callen's instructions, Cannon added that Budenz's allegations "do not apply to this particular person or to anyone else who ever worked in the National Office of the Socialist Workers Party." He said, falsely, that the "Control Commission rejected the accusation and exonerated the accused comrade, who had fully cooperated with the investigation, answered all questions put to her and supplied the Control Commission with all the data relating to her biography and previous occupations, which were subject to verification."[40]

In fact, none of Callen's claims had been verified nor had there been any real investigation. From the initial visit of Shachtman and Glotzer to the issuing of the Control Commission's findings, little more than two weeks had elapsed. Callen had not cooperated with the SWP.

Budenz was not through with his exposure of Callen. On November 11, 1950, Budenz submitted an affidavit to the House Un-American Activities Committee that included new details of Sylvia Callen-Caldwell's role. This time, Budenz dispensed with the use of the fictional name "Helen."

"Another person whom I introduced to Roberts," Budenz testified, referencing the alias for Dr. Gregory Rabinowitz "was Sylvia Caulwell [sic] and whose maiden name was something like Sylvia Kallen [sic]."

> Her husband, Irving Franklin, had been in Spain working in secret work and had been sent to Canada to aid in espionage

---

39. Ibid.

40. The *Militant*, August 28, 1950, available at https://www.marxists.org/history/etol/news-pape/themilitant/1950/v14n35-aug-28-1950-mil.pdf

activities there ... Sylvia Franklin under the direction of Roberts-Rabinowitz, gradually made herself indispensable to James Cannon, then head of the American Trotskyites. She became his secretary and served in that capacity for some time. Roberts-Rabinowitz advised me that she had proved to be invaluable.[41]

The SWP did not respond to this testimony.

Joseph Hansen and the SWP cover-up

Over the next years, the evidence against Franklin mounted and the SWP continued to defend her along the lines Franklin laid out in her meeting with Dobbs, repeated in Cannon's article of August 28, 1950.

In 1954 and again in 1958, Franklin testified before federal grand juries investigating Soviet espionage in the US. In her first appearance, Franklin relied on her Fifth Amendment right to remain silent. In 1958, however, she admitted that she was, in fact, a GPU agent. This testimony would not be known for another twenty-five years.

In 1959, however, the journalist Isaac Don Levine published an account of Ramon Mercader and the GPU's assassination of Trotsky, *The Mind of An Assassin*, that substantiated Budenz's testimony.

Levine wrote:

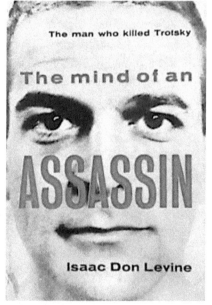

He [Budenz] made it possible for the NKVD [the GPU] to steam open and pilfer Trotsky's mail to his New York followers. He got a Communist Party girl, a Chicago social worker, to move to New York and volunteer her services to James Cannon, the American

The cover of Isaac Don Levine's book on Trotsky's killer, Ramon Mercader

---

41. *The Sylvia Franklin Dossier* (New York: Labor Publications Inc., 1977).

Trotskyist leader: "She had the full run of the Trotskyite offices, became Cannon's Secretary, and made available to the Soviet secret police all the correspondence with Trotsky in Mexico City and with other Trotskyites throughout the world," he testified.[42]

SWP leader Joseph Hansen tried to convince Levine to drop the matter. Hansen wrote to Cannon on October 24, 1958 about a discussion he had with Levine about the latter's book:

> What he wanted from me was information on any spies or evidence of spies in Soviet pay working in or around our movement. Not having any such information, I could not help him; in fact, when he came to Sylvia Caldwell I hope I was able to give him some further considerations to help squelch that rumor.[43]

Joseph Hansen

On March 19, 1960, Hansen responded to an urgent note from Gerry Healy, then National Secretary of the Socialist Labour League, the British section of the International Committee of the Fourth International. Healy inquired from Hansen what the latter knew about a report in Levine's book regarding another GPU agent, named "Etienne," the party name of Mark Zborowski, the Paris-based GPU agent who played a central role in providing the Stalinist secret police with information that led to the murders of Trotsky's son Lev Sedov, Trotsky's political secretary Erwin Wolf, soon-to-be Secretary of the Fourth International Rudolf Klement, and GPU defector Ignatz Reiss, who left the Soviet Union to join the Fourth International.

Referencing his own review of Levine's book, Hansen attempted to deflect Healy's interest in Etienne, claiming the SWP could not spare anyone to attend Etienne-Zborowski's 1958 perjury trial, where the agent was sentenced to prison for lying under oath about his ties to Jack Soble, a GPU

---

42. Ibid.

43. Joseph Hansen to James P. Cannon, October 24, 1958, *Wisconsin Historical Society*.

Rudolf Klement, Irwin Wolf, Ignatz Reiss and Leon Sedov—all murdered by the GPU

controller responsible for a network of agents in the United States. In reality, Hansen and the SWP had no interest in covering a trial that could expose details of GPU infiltration of the Fourth International.

Hansen said he "decided not to give much space to the Etienne case" in his review of *The Mind of An Assassin* because, in his words, Levine was an anticommunist. Hansen said he considered referencing "the report about Cannon's personal secretary being a GPU agent" as an example of Levine's false material, adding, "But this would necessitate an article on our investigation years ago of the slander and the review would have been thrown out of balance."

Hansen continued, "One of our primary concerns was not to give the slightest encouragement to the view Levine seeks to implant—that our organizations are loaded with spies. Such a view is deadly poisonous and can do incomparably greater harm than the occasional stool pigeon that turns up in any organization."[44]

Weeks later, in April 1960, Cannon wrote a letter from Los Angeles to his wife, Rose Karsner, which is published here for the first time. In a discouraged tone, Cannon wrote:

> I haven't felt like writing but I am sending this note so that you won't worry about something possibly being wrong.
>
> ...But spiritually I am tired and have no present ambition to *do* anything. I spend the time reading stuff that is easy to read, thinking a little, but mostly musing and remembering and reflecting. Most of my musing and remembering these days is sad, and that paralyzes the will to work or even to plan to work later on.
>
> The memories of the work I have already done in the past—not speaking and writing, which was the easiest part and

---

44. *The Indictment Stands* (New York: Labor Publications, Inc. 1976).

probably all that others really noticed, but carrying people on my back—give me a delayed reaction of spiritual weariness. I feel that I have done all of that heavy work I can do or even want to do again for anybody...

I don't want to *do* anything for anybody—in fact, I can't— and I don't want anybody to try to do anything for me except for routine technical things. The most I want from people now is to let me alone, not pull at me or try to push me, and above all not expect me [to] pick them up and inspire them and try to solve their problems."[45]

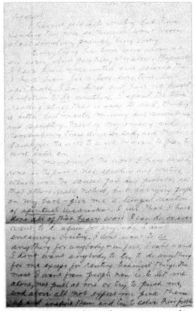

Cannon's letter to his wife, Rose Karsner (See Appendix B, pp. 165–166)

That same year Sylvia Callen was named as an unindicted co-conspirator in the indictment of GPU spy Robert Soblen, Jack Soble's brother. At Soblen's trial, further information proving Callen's role emerged. Soble testified, "I went further into the Trotsky field and worked with the secretary of Cannon, Sylvia ... also introduced to me by the same Russians who worked for them already before ... She gathered material at the secretariat of Cannon and gave it to me ... pure Trotsky material."[46]

The SWP again failed to cover the trial and report on this testimony. The absence of any coverage by the *Militant* of the Soblen trial—which was front page news in *The New York Times*—is all the more incriminating given the fact that another prominent ex-member of the SWP, Floyd Cleveland Miller, was also listed as a GPU co-conspirator.

The cover-up of Callen's role as a GPU agent became the official policy of the SWP leadership. In a manner that defies innocent explanation, the SWP went out of its way to uphold her bona fides, perpetuating the myth of Cannon's selfless secretary and denouncing Budenz as a perjurer.

---

45. James P. Cannon to Rose Karsner, April 1960, *Wisconsin Historical Society*
46. *The Gelfand Case* vol. 1 (Detroit: Labor Publications, 1985) p. 58.

GPU agents Jack Soble and Robert Soblen

On November 12, 1966, Cannon wrote to Reba Hansen, Joseph Hansen's wife, regarding a proposal by a party member to change the functioning of the SWP's Control Commission. He addressed the matter in a thoroughly dishonest way.

Cannon explained that the party's Control Commission was responsible for the "double purpose" of maintaining party security and "to provide the maximum assurance that any individual party member, accused or rumored to be unworthy of party membership, could be assured of the fullest investigation..."[47]

To defend his position, Cannon cited the case of Callen without identifying her by name. He said that at the time, "a rumor circulated by the Shachtmanites and others outside the party against the integrity of a National Office secretarial worker was thoroughly investigated by the Control Commission which, after taking stenographic testimony from all available sources, declared the rumors unfounded and cleared the accused party member to continue her work."[48]

This letter to Reba Hansen had clearly been written for public consumption, with the purpose of suppressing questions about the official story, particularly among older members of the SWP who must have wondered why Sylvia Callen had suddenly left the party.

---

47. *Building the Revolutionary Party, an Introduction to James P. Cannon* (Chippendale, Australia: New Course Publications, 1997) p.70.
48. Ibid., p. 71.

A two-page spread from the ICFI's "Case for a Commission of Inquiry" on the Budenz revelations

Cannon's letter neglected to explain that Callen was not simply "a National Office secretarial worker," but his personal secretary, assistant and his wife's close friend. He hid the fact that she quit the party shortly after supposedly being cleared "to continue her work." The 1947 Control Commission did not investigate the matter "thoroughly" and it did not take testimony "from all available sources," as he claimed. Her lies were exposed by Budenz, Levine and Soble, and the SWP Control Commission covered up her real role.

The SWP defends Hansen and Franklin

In May 1975, the International Committee initiated its own investigation into *Security and the Fourth International*. The initial findings included evidence of Hansen's meetings with the FBI and State Department as well as information of Callen's role as a GPU agent.

Hansen denounced the revelations as "A Geyser of Mud." He wrote that "the Healyites in no place indicate the basis of their charge that McGregor was 'an FBI agent who was operating under diplomatic cover at the American

Embassy.' ... it is sufficient to note how the Healyites use this label to suggest that at Coyoacan I was in 'association' with an agent of the FBI."[49]

Hansen rejected the ICFI's call for a commission of inquiry into Trotsky's assassination, adding:

> Sylvia Caldwell (that was her party name) worked very hard in her rather difficult assignment of managing the national office of the Socialist Workers party, which included helping Cannon in a secretarial capacity. In fact all the comrades who shared these often irksome chores with her regarded her as exemplary. They burned as much as she did over the foul slander spread by Budenz.[50]

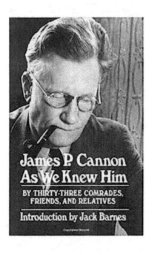

In the December 8, 1975 edition of the SWP magazine *Intercontinental Press*, leading SWP member George Novack attacked Healy's "reckless and indiscriminate allegations" against "Sylvia Caldwell, Cannon's secretary," writing that "Anything goes in his frantic endeavors to cast a net of suspicion around Joseph Hansen and his colleagues."[51]

In early 1976, the SWP published a collection of essays memorializing the life of James P. Cannon, who had died in August 1974. Titled *James P. Cannon As We Knew Him*, the volume consisted of essays written by SWP members, including one by Joseph Hansen's wife, Reba Hansen, which contained the following extraordinary tribute:

> During those years Sylvia Caldwell served as secretary in the national office, a job that included working with Jim, who held the post of national secretary. She was the second full-time secretary the party had. The first was Lillian Roberts.
>
> Jim often told us about how it was "in the old days," when it was difficult to get things done because of having no secretarial

49. *Intercontinental Press*, November 24, 1975, vol. 13 no. 42, page 1643.

50. Ibid.

51. George Novack, "Healy's Frame-up Against Joseph Hansen," *Intercontinental Press*, December 8, 1975, vol. 13 no. 44, p. 1710.

help. He said he was grateful for any help he could get and he never failed to show his deep appreciation for the aid that Sylvia gave.

Jim was fond of telling the story about how Sylvia went to a business school to learn shorthand when it was proposed she work in the national office. This was before the days of the tape recorder, and shorthand was essential to taking adequate minutes at meetings and dictation for letters and articles. Sylvia learned fast and well. Her Gregg characters were like copper-plate engravings, her typing without strike-overs, and no messy erasures.

When the load in the national office was heavy and Sylvia needed help, I gave her a hand, working very closely with her. Her efficiency impressed me. She knew how to do everything that was necessary to keep a one-person office running smoothly. Her devotion to the movement and her readiness to put in long hours of hard work inspired us all.

Sylvia and I became close collaborators and good personal friends. She was a warm human being.

When Sylvia left New York in 1947 because of family obligations, Jim asked me to take her place in the national office. Since this included working closely with Jim, I felt a little nervous, but Sylvia helped me through the transition from business manager of the *Militant* to my new assignment.

At that time Rose and Jim lived at 126 West Eleventh Street, seventh floor. The apartment building was modern—it had an elevator—and the rooms were large by New York standards. The front room, facing on Eleventh Street, was big enough for two desks, several filing cabinets, and a worktable. Sylvia took me there to work with her and learn the ropes.

But Jim didn't shift easily from one secretary to another. And it was only after Sylvia had been gone some time that Jim felt enough at home with me through working together in the national office to ask me to come over to West Eleventh Street.[52]

There is no innocent explanation for the inclusion of this lying tribute to Sylvia Callen in a book that was supposedly intended to eulogize Cannon.

---

52. *James P. Cannon as We Knew Him* (New York: Pathfinder Press, 1976) p. 232–33.

Reba Hansen knew full well that Callen had suddenly disappeared from the SWP national office in 1947 not because of "family obligations," but because she had been exposed as a GPU agent. Her gratuitous tribute to Cannon's secretary, who had for nearly a decade managed the national office, did not make any mention whatever of the allegations made by Budenz, the 1947 Control Commission, Budenz's more detailed account in 1950 of Callen's activities, or of her being named by the US government as a co-conspirator in the 1960 trial of Soviet agent Robert Soblen.

The ICFI locates Sylvia Callen

The SWP's defense of Callen made it critical to locate the former agent. In 1976, the Workers League (predecessor of the Socialist Equality Party), initiated a search to find Callen. Without the benefit of modern-day search engines, it was necessary to reconstruct the biography of this dedicated and ruthless American GPU agent, who was able to spy on and betray without remorse people with whom she worked on a daily basis for almost a decade. She was absolutely indifferent to the human impact, which included murder, of her actions.

In order to locate Callen it was necessary to discover the name under which she was living. The November 1960 federal indictment that named her as a co-conspirator in the GPU spy ring led by Robert Soblen and Jack Soble identified her only by her maiden name, Callen. However, through an examination of court documents, David North, the national secretary of the Workers League, was able to ascertain that Callen had been living in Wheaton, Illinois, at the time of her indictment.

Callen left Wheaton shortly after the conclusion of the Soblen trial, but left a paper trail that could be followed. In the early 1950s Callen had divorced her husband and co-GPU agent, Zalmond Franklin, who died in 1958. Callen married her second husband, James Doxsee, a member or fellow-traveler of the Communist Party who worked for ABC. Together they had three children, whom they raised in Wheaton. Her pleasant middle-class life was disturbed only by visits from the FBI and two extensive federal grand jury testimonies, the first in 1954 and the second in 1958.

After selling their home in Wheaton, James and Sylvia Doxsee relocated to a nearby West Chicago suburb. The domesticated Mrs. Doxsee was careful to conceal her past, refusing to allow her family and few friends to take pictures of her. In the mid-1970s, the Doxsees sold their home and purchased an RV, which became their mobile residence. Much of their time was spent driving through Central America.

However, in May 1977 the Doxsees returned to Wheaton to visit James' aging mother. North had been able to establish Callen's new married name. He learned in advance of the Doxsees' planned visit to Wheaton, where they had reserved a space for their RV in a local trailer park. He and Alex Mitchell, who was then the editor of the *News Line*, the publication of the Workers Revolutionary

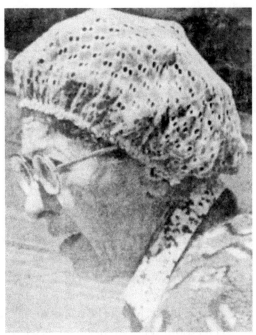

GPU agent Sylvia Callen/Franklin/Caldwell/Doxsee, pictured in Wheaton, IL in 1977 (photo by David North)

Party (British section of the International Committee), located Sylvia Callen-Franklin-Caldwell-Doxsee at this trailer park in Wheaton.

On May 9, 1977, North and Mitchell went to the Doxsees' trailer and confronted the ex-GPU spy.

When asked about her political past, Doxsee (aka Callen, Caldwell, Franklin) acknowledged working as Cannon's secretary, but sought to brush aside her years in the SWP as a minor episode in her life. As the *Bulletin*, newspaper of the Workers League, reported on May 31, 1977, Doxsee said: "I don't see why it's even important. I was never really in politics. I never read. I never understood it. I was just an immature child, that's about all I can say. ... It's like I blacked it out. All that period of my life."[53]

Regarding James P. Cannon, with whom she had closely worked on a day-by-day basis for almost a decade, Doxsee said with unconcealed contempt, "He wasn't an important man, in my opinion. Is he? What part did he play in the world?"

---

53. *The Sylvia Franklin Dossier*, (New York: Labor Publications Inc., 1977).

Pressed by North and Mitchell to explain why she was indicted as a co-conspirator in a GPU spy ring, Doxsee feigned amnesia. The following exchange was reported in the *Bulletin*:

> Question: This is an official document. Grand Jury, 1960, in which your name is mentioned right here, Sylvia Callen.
> Franklin: Grand Jury charges!
> Question: Yes. All I would like to ask you is why were you named on this indictment? That's all I'd like to ask you.
> Franklin: I can't believe it!

Another document was shown to her.

> Question: Here as well is your name on the list of witnesses the Government was going to call.
> Franklin: My God!
> Question: You have no explanation for your name.
> Franklin: No, but the FBI came to see me here.
> Question: Why did they come to see you?
> Franklin: I don't know. I had a mental breakdown afterwards so it must have been pretty terrible.
> Question: So why...
> Franklin: I don't know. I don't know. I don't want to think about it.
> Question: Do you have a memory block which begins after all these events supposedly took place?
> Franklin: I don't know. I wish you wouldn't try to make me remember because I'll have a breakdown. I can't remember. It's been many years, and I've put it out of my mind.
> Question: Is it possible that you were in the Communist Party and simply have forgotten all about it?
> Franklin: I don't know. I don't know. It could be one way. It could be the other. I can't believe that person was me. I can't believe that I worked in that office. That I was his secretary. I can't believe anything.[54]

After the publication of the interview with Sylvia Doxsee-Franklin-Caldwell-Callen on May 31, 1977, Hansen responded in an *Intercontinental*

---

54. Ibid.

Reba and Joseph Hansen hiding from the camera (photo by David North)

Press article on June 20, 1977 titled "Healyites Escalate Frame-up of Trotskyist Leaders." In the article, Hansen attempted to cast doubt on what he called the "purported" interview, stating that the ICFI had "escalated their slanders of the leadership of the Socialist Workers party."[55]

Hansen attacked the *Security and the Fourth International* investigation by referencing the 1947 Control Commission:

> The members of this select body of witch-hunters [i.e., the ICFI] commit themselves to a slander they had previously only hinted at; namely, that the control commission set up by the Socialist Workers party in 1947 to examine the rumors circulating about Caldwell was "rigged."

He continued:

> If there was a coverup, if the control commission was rigged, if no control commission was held at all—as the Healyites now allege—then the main guilt clearly falls on James P. Cannon, one of the founders of the Fourth International. In accordance with

---

55. Joseph Hansen, "Healyites Escalate Frame-up of Trotskyist Leaders," *Intercontinental Press*, June 20, 1977, vol. 15 no. 23, p. 700.

the logic of the Big Lie as practiced by the Healyites, Cannon must be listed as an "accomplice of the GPU," if not worse.

This is only the beginning. If Cannon was an "accomplice" or "agent" of the GPU, then the entire top leadership of the SWP associated with him must be similarly listed, for they obviously participated in staging the alleged control commission fraud, whether by helping to rig it or, if it was not held at all, by making out—along with Cannon—that it *had* been held.

How far back did such fraudulent practices go? Was Cannon an accomplice or agent of the GPU when he founded American Trotskyism? When he collaborated with Trotsky in founding the Fourth International? Was his long battle against Stalinism a sham? Were his close relations with Trotsky a cover-up for a secret connection with Stalin? Just whom did Cannon use as willing tools in working for the GPU—for instance, in the alleged fake control commission?[56]

On June 25, 1977, North, in an article titled "Hansen's Big Lie Grows Bigger" published in the *News Line,* responded to Hansen's claims. After quoting the above paragraphs, North wrote:

> All this comes straight from the pen of Joseph Hansen! He is charged with covering up the activities of GPU agents, and so he replies by trying to frighten SWP members with the suggestion that his guilt makes Cannon a Stalinist agent! He is trying to intimidate the SWP membership and bully them into silence by telling them how terrible the consequences will be if the International Committee's charges against him are proven correct.
>
> Hansen deals with his members like an airplane hijacker with a bomb in his hand who waves it above his head and shouts at the passengers: "Anyone tries to stop me and we'll all be blown to Kingdom come!"
>
> What is clear is that Hansen will stop at nothing to save his own political neck. Hansen is not protecting Cannon; he is using him to save himself.[57]

---

56. Ibid.
57. *Sylvia Franklin Dossier.*

Tom Henehan, 26-year-old member of the Workers League Political Committee, murdered in 1977 after Hansen warned of "deadly consequences" to Security and the Fourth International investigation

The fact that Hansen resorted to this desperate method precisely on the question of the 1947 Control Commission shows just how central it was to Hansen's "narrative." As North wrote:

This is Hansen at his tricks again. He doesn't give a straightforward answer, backed with evidence, to the question: was the SWP control commission rigged or wasn't it? Instead, he drags in James P. Cannon in order to hide behind his grave. Why doesn't he leave Cannon out of it? The International Committee has made no accusations against Cannon. We've accused Hansen! It's Hansen's favourite trick to immediately conjure up Cannon's ghost the moment he himself is challenged.[58]

The publication of the ICFI's interview with Sylvia Callen-Doxsee and the calling into question of the 1947 Control Commission produced anxiety among the SWP leadership and the Stalinist bureaucracy. Those involved in penetrating the Trotskyist movement had good reason to believe the *Security and the Fourth International* investigation would publish further revelations exposing the GPU infiltration of the Trotskyist movement.

Hansen responded by adopting the methods of Stalinist intimidation, attempting to create a threatening atmosphere of provocation against the ICFI. Unable to challenge the damning implications of the Callen interview, Hansen wrote, "[T]he Healyites are quite capable of initiating physical

---

58. Ibid.

violence against other sectors of the labor movement..." In the same article, he threatened the International Committee, warning it that *Security and the Fourth International* would bring "deadly consequences."[59]

Less than four months later, on October 16, 1977, Tom Henehan, a twenty-six-year-old member of the Workers League Political Committee, was assassinated in New York City by two professional gunmen while supervising a public party event. Though the killers were quickly identified, the New York police refused to make any arrests. Finally, after a three-year campaign waged by the Workers League, the gunmen were arrested, placed on trial, and convicted in July 1981 of second-degree murder. Following the trial, the private detective who had investigated the case for the defense attorney informed North that "the word on the street" was that the killing was a "hit."

The Callen grand jury transcripts

In August 1977, Alan Gelfand, an SWP member and a public defender in Los Angeles, obtained copies of the *Security and the Fourth International* documents circulated by Workers League members outside the SWP's National Convention in Oberlin, Ohio.[60]

Gelfand asked other SWP members about the documents and particularly the 1940 State Department and FBI memos that referenced Hansen's meeting with the GPU and with the US government.

In response, Gelfand was given different explanations. Some SWP members told him the documents were forgeries, either by the Workers League or the FBI. Others believed the documents to be legitimate, but they assumed there existed a reasonable explanation. SWP National Secretary Jack Barnes, however, made it a point to approach Gelfand, verified to him the authenticity of the documents, and further explained to him that they referred to when Hansen was instructed by the party to contact the government in order to tap all sources of information concerning the assassination. Moreover, he told Gelfand that Hansen would be publishing this explanation shortly. Neither Hansen nor any other SWP leader ever published any such reply.

When no reply was issued in the months that followed, Gelfand raised his concerns with members in Los Angeles and was advised by various party leaders

59. *Intercontinental Press*, June 20, 1977.

60. For a complete review of the chronological events leading up to the Gelfand Case, see *The Gelfand Case*, vol. 1 (Detroit: Labor Publications, 1985), pp. 35–102.

that all the allegations made by the International Committee had been fully answered in a party internal bulletin that was provocatively titled, "Healy's Big Lie."

Gelfand then carefully studied this internal bulletin and concluded that the answers were contradicted by documents uncovered by the *Security and the Fourth International* investigation after its publication.

Gelfand continued to ask for discussion regarding Hansen's connections to the GPU and United States agencies, and of Callen's connections to the GPU. The SWP leadership repeatedly barred him from speaking to

EDUCATION FOR SOCIALISTS

ISSUED BY THE NATIONAL EDUCATION DEPARTMENT SOCIALIST WORKERS PARTY 14 CHARLES LANE NEW YORK, N.Y. 10014

HEALY'S BIG LIE

The Slander Campaign Against Joseph Hansen, George Novack, and the Fourth International

Statements and Articles by:
• Joseph Hansen • George Novack
• John and Mary Archer
• George Breitman • Charles
Curtiss • Sam Gordon • Betty
Hamilton • C.L.R. James • Pierre
Lambert • Bala Tampoe • Ernest
Tate • Charles Van Gelderen
•Jean Van Heijenoort • 'Nea
Poreia' • 'Red Weekly' • 'Socialist
Action' • 'Socialist Press'

DECEMBER 1976 $2.00, £ .60

"Healy's Big Lie." The SWP mobilized the international Pabloite movement to slander Security and the Fourth International

other members about his concerns. Gelfand realized that the cover-up must be tied to the activity of high level state agents still operating within the party.

In December 1978, Gelfand filed an *amicus curiae* brief in support of a lawsuit by the SWP related to the FBI's surveillance of the movement through COINTELPRO. This lawsuit, which had been initiated by the SWP primarily as a fundraising activity, was not being conducted with the intention of exposing past or still active agents inside the party. In fact, the US government eventually settled the case by paying the SWP hundreds of thousands of dollars but without identifying a single agent that it had infiltrated into the party. In the course of the trial, the FBI admitted that between 1960 and 1976 there were three hundred informants serving as members of the SWP.

Gelfand's brief, however, referenced the history of FBI and GPU penetration of the movement, and the recent revelations concerning Callen and Hansen to further demonstrate the need for the court to compel the government to identify the agents that had been sent into the SWP.

This demand outraged the SWP leadership, which accused Gelfand of violating party discipline. On January 5, 1979, SWP National Secretary Jack Barnes charged Gelfand with "undisciplined and disloyal behavior." Six days later, on January 11, the SWP Political Committee expelled him. This was the last meeting of the SWP Political Committee attended by Joseph Hansen. He died in New York City exactly one week later, on January 18, 1979. Hansen was sixty-eight years old.

In a letter to the SWP Political Committee, dated January 29, 1979, Gelfand stated that he had been purged from the SWP to block the exposure of agents inside the party. "This purge," he wrote, "is the result of my persistent and principled fight over the last eighteen months to obtain satisfactory answers and explanations to the various questions raised by Joseph Hansen's and Sylvia Franklin's relationship with the FBI and GPU."

On July 18, 1979 Gelfand filed a lawsuit in federal court in Los Angeles, alleging that the government violated his First Amendment rights by infiltrating the SWP with agents who expelled him from the political party of his choosing.

THE GELFAND CASE

A LEGAL HISTORY OF
THE EXPOSURE OF
U.S. GOVERNMENT AGENTS
IN THE LEADERSHIP OF THE
SOCIALIST WORKERS PARTY

VOLUME I

The Gelfand Case, the record of Gelfand v. Attorney General, published by the International Committee of the Fourth International in 1985

Gelfand named as defendants high US government officials—including the attorney general and the directors of the FBI and CIA—as well as leading members of the Socialist Workers Party.

The SWP immediately filed a motion to dismiss Gelfand's lawsuit. Oral arguments were made before United States District Judge Mariana R. Pfaelzer on November 19, 1979.

In June 1980 Pfaelzer denied the SWP's motion, finding that Gelfand's complaint raised fundamental constitutional issues. She wrote that "the government manipulation and takeover of plaintiff's political party that is alleged ... is a drastic interference with the associational rights of its adherents and cannot pass constitutional muster."[61]

Gelfand and his lawyers took depositions of many current and former SWP members. The first to be deposed was Sylvia Callen, who had relocated

---

61. Ibid., p. 111.

to an exclusive neighborhood along Chicago's "Gold Coast." In the course of her deposition, she invoked memory loss 231 times. She admitted, however, during the course of the deposition that she had previously appeared before at least two federal grand juries. Referencing her grand jury testimony, Callen said:

> Q: Did you take the Fifth Amendment on any questions?
> A: On some I did.
> Q: How did you know to take the Fifth Amendment?
> A: From reading the papers from the McCarthy's thing. I copied it down, even what to say.
> Q: Did you talk to anybody about when to use the Fifth Amendment?
> A: No. I probably should have, but I'm just so dumb.
> Q: What types of areas did you take the Fifth Amendment in?
> A: Oh, I don't remember.
> Q: Well, would it be fair to say that certain questions you were willing to answer?
> A: I don't remember.
> Q: Well, did you answer any questions?
> A: That I don't remember either. Maybe I didn't answer any questions, I don't know.[62]

Although grand jury proceedings are generally sealed, Gelfand's attorneys petitioned a federal court in New York to release the transcripts of Sylvia Callen's testimony of 1954 and 1958. This request was bitterly opposed by the SWP, which argued for continued secrecy on the basis that the "grand jury testimony is wholly irrelevant to any material issue in this litigation" and "should not be disclosed."

The judge in New York released the transcripts to Judge Pfaelzer in Los Angeles. Pfaelzer, a liberal Democratic judge, was managing the case with extreme caution.

Her ruling in June 1980 had accepted that Gelfand's expulsion from the SWP would be unconstitutional if engineered by government agents to prevent their own expulsion. However, as the case proceeded, Pfaelzer, the SWP, and the government sought to block Gelfand from accessing the evidence he

---

62. Deposition of Sylvia Doxsee, taken September 22, 1980, *Gelfand v. Smith et al.*, p. 104.

would need to prove that his First Amendment right was denied by the government agents who expelled him from the SWP.

As Gelfand and his attorneys wrote in their closing brief on summary judgment:

> Legally, this case presents a double paradox. For the court, there is the tension between the enforcement of First Amendment rights on the one hand and the duty to protect claims of national security on the other. In denying the motions to dismiss, the court in ringing terms affirmed the right to political association free from governmental interference. By upholding the government's claim of informer privilege on plaintiff's motion to compel, however, the court demonstrated its sensitivity to the countervailing concerns. Rarely does a case require the reconciliation of two such fundamentally opposing legal principles.
>
> The plaintiff faces the other side of the coin. On the one hand he is told that, if he can prove that the leaders of the Party are agents of the United States government, he will establish the violation of his constitutional rights. Yet the most straightforward method of proof—examination of relevant government documents and direct responses to questions aimed at government agencies—has been denied to him.[63]

Pfaelzer appeared concerned that Gelfand's evidence-gathering efforts would lead to the publication of state secrets regarding the penetration of the SWP. When denying Gelfand's request that Zborowski be compelled to testify, she said:

> Now, my feeling is that Mr. Zborowski, given the very nature of this case, when postured up against, since the case was filed, an enactment known as the Protection of Certain National Security Information, which has just become law this year, does or would run a possible risk of violating section 601(a) of that act, were he asked to identify either by name or description or anything else which might lead to the identity of possible

---

63. *The Gelfand Case*, vol. 1, pp. 174–75.

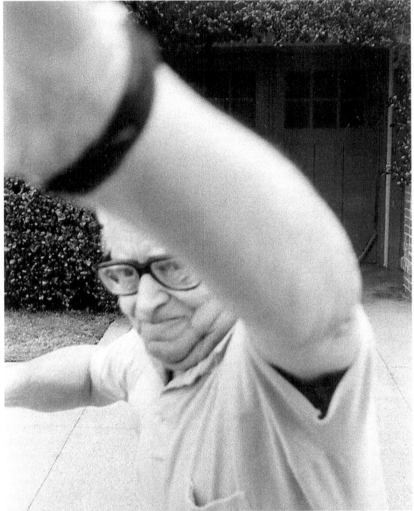

Mark Zborowski, alias "Etienne," was located in San Francisco in August 1975 by the International Committee of the Fourth International (Photo by David North)

intelligence agents who might be superficially participating in this Socialist Workers Party.

And that act specifically provides that if any person has such information and knowingly discloses it, regardless of whatever the motivation, can be prosecuted, fined $50,000, and imprisoned up to ten years. And, therefore, I feel that his invoking the Fifth Amendment in that area, which is the pivotal point of this lawsuit, perhaps, nonetheless is a legitimate concern of the witness and his counsel that must be honored by this court. And, therefore, insofar as any invocation of the Fifth Amendment that has, up to now, been asserted in this deposition, I'm not going to order him to further answer.[64]

The highest levels of the US government and military-intelligence apparatus were closely monitoring the case. A June 11, 1982 memorandum from Central Intelligence Agency General Counsel Stanley Sporkin to CIA Director William J. Casey cites the Gelfand case as an "item of major interest" for the CIA.

Referencing a request by Gelfand and his attorneys that the CIA and other state agencies reveal the identities of agents in the party, the recently-declassified CIA memo reads:

Recently declassified CIA memo protecting the agency's "statutory exemption from any requirement to disclose names or functions of CIA personnel..." (See Appendix B, p. 169)

In Gelfand v. Attorney General, DCI, et al., Gelfand claims that alleged CIA and FBI agents in the Socialist Workers Party (SWP) expelled him from the party. In pretrial discovery, Gelfand submitted interrogatories asking the DCI [Director of Central Intelligence] whether 19 named SWP members are or have been CIA agents and whether CIA believes that one named individual is a Soviet intelligence agent. The DCI refused to answer the interrogatories on the ground that answering them would tend to reveal intelligence activities, sources, and methods. The

---

64. *The Gelfand Case*, vol. 2 (Detroit: Labor Publications, 1985), p. 469.

U.S. District Court hearing the case upheld the DCI's refusal to answer, holding that the DCI's statutory responsibility to protect intelligence sources and methods and the CIA's statutory exemption from any requirement to disclose the names or functions of CIA personnel justify the refusal to answer.[65]

Jack Barnes, National Secretary of the Socialist Workers Party

Under pressure from the government, Pfaelzer sought to restrict the focus of the trial to the narrow procedural issue of whether Gelfand technically violated party rules by continuing to press for answers on the Hansen and Callen exposures after the SWP leadership told him to stop.

Before the trial, Gelfand's attorney, John Burton, asked Judge Pfaelzer to release the transcripts of the Callen grand jury transcripts that had been forwarded from New York. The judge replied that she would rule later on that request. Several further requests for the release of the transcripts, before and during the trial itself, were brushed aside. Her brusque demeanor and seemingly hostile attitude to Gelfand gave the impression that she would eventually deny the request altogether.

On the last day of the trial, March 9, 1983, SWP National Secretary Barnes was called to testify. Apparently confident that Pfaelzer would not release the grand jury transcripts, Barnes concluded his testimony with an extraordinary tribute to this GPU agent:

> Q: Now, was it your opinion at the time you received [Gelfand's letter] that there was no evidence whatsoever to indicate that Sylvia Franklin was an agent of the GPU?

---

65. Declassified CIA memo from General Counsel Stanley Sporkin to CIA Director William Casey, June 11, 1982.

A: All the evidence is just the opposite. Her whole comportment not only when she was in the movement but everything that's happened since she left indicates that she is exactly what she was: a loyal, hard-working, and model member of our movement.

Q: That is still your opinion today?

A: Well, my opinion today is she is one of my heroes after the harassment and what she's been through the last couple of years. I would even feel more strongly about her, her character, than I did then.

Q: Now, was Sylvia Franklin the subject of an SWP Control Commission investigation?

A: No. Sylvia Franklin was not the subject of an SWP Control Commission. Sylvia Caldwell was invited to an SWP Control Commission hearing to discuss the fact of the Shachtmanites were spreading this rumor. The control commission had their hearing and then they passed a motion saying, one, that there is zero evidence that there is anything connected with this rumor that could be true and, number two, which of course is the key of why they met, to request of the Shachtmanites to cease spreading this rumor because of that.[66]

These lies may have proved too much for Pfaelzer. Following Barnes' testimony, and after Gelfand's attorneys announced they had no further evidence to present, Pfaelzer suddenly released the transcripts of both the 1954 and 1958 grand jury hearings. While Pfaelzer shielded Barnes from exposure on the witness stand, these transcripts nevertheless decisively answered, with Callen's own words, the question of her role as a GPU agent inside the SWP.

In her 1954 testimony, Callen employed the tactic that she would later use when confronted by North and Mitchell in 1977 and during her 1980 deposition, i.e., memory loss. In 1954, Callen did confirm that she had been married to Franklin, and that they had attended meetings of the Stalinist Young Communist League. But in response to crucial questions, such as whether she had met with Louis Budenz, Callen stated: "I can't answer that because of possible self-incrimination," invoking her Fifth Amendment privilege.[67]

---

66. *The Gelfand Case*, vol. 2, pp. 635–36.
67. *The Confession of Sylvia Franklin* (Detroit: Labor Publications Inc., 1983) p. 19.

In her second grand jury appearance, on June 18, 1958, Callen was more forthcoming. She realized that the grand jury was preparing indictments for an espionage case against her former GPU handler, Robert Soblen, and that she was facing the danger of a lengthy prison term, if not the death penalty, on charges of treason.

The US government attorney began his interrogation by reminding Callen (now addressed as "Mrs. Doxsee") of problems that arose during her 1954 appearance:

> Q. You do recall testifying before a Grand Jury?
> A. Oh, yes.
> Q. And you do recall, Mrs. Doxsee, that at that time your memory was not as good as it might be?
> A. Yes.
> Q. And have you since that time tried to improve your memory as best as you could?
> A. Yes, I have.
> Q. And have you talked over the matters with your husband?
> A. Yes.
> Q. And do you feel that you are beginning to remember some things that you had difficulty with before.
> A. Yes.[68]

Callen told the story of her role as an agent inside the SWP. She recalled how she was paid to hand over confidential information from the desk of James Cannon to two leading GPU spies, Dr. Gregory Rabinowitz—the "Roberts" Budenz worked with—and Jack Soble, the brother of Robert Soblen. Under examination by a government attorney, the transcript of her testimony read, in part:

> Q: If I can make a little resume here, Miss Doxsee, you say then that you joined the Young Communist League in the middle thirties, but after you joined the Young Communist League and at the suggestion from someone from the Communist Party you joined an organization that was part of the Social Workers' [sic] organization. Is that right?

---

68. Ibid., p. 23.

A: I think that's it.

Q: Then ultimately you entered the office of James Cannon and became his secretary?

A: Yes.

Q: Now, during the time that you were working in Mr. Cannon's office, did you ever discuss anything that you learned there with anybody else?

A: Yes.

Q: Do you recall who it was that you discussed that with?

A: Well, I used to go to my former husband's apartment, Zalmond's apartment.

Q: Did you meet anyone there?

A: I met—not every time I went up there—but I had met a man I called Jack [Jack was the alias used by Gregory Rabinowitz— aka Roberts—during his meetings with Sylvia Franklin]. I don't know his name.

...

Q: This man, Jack, you say, was introduced to you by Louis Budenz?

A: Yes.

Q: And that was in Chicago?

A: Yes, that's the way I recall it.

Q: Do you ever recall meeting a woman to whom you gave information?

A: Yes; a woman's apartment.

Q: And was that a different apartment from the apartment you have previously described?

A: Yes.[69]

Callen was referring to the apartment of Stalinist agent Lucy Booker. She then testified, "I used to go up there and type reports also, the way I used to at my husband's apartment, and sometimes, as I recall, she was there and sometimes she wasn't just as I recall."

There, she would sometimes meet Jack Soble, who she knew as "Sam." He would pay her for her services.

---

69. Ibid., pp. 25–27.

Q: Do you recall how you knew—commenced going to this apartment that you're now describing, the woman's apartment?

A: No, I don't.

Q: Did someone tell you to go there?

A: No, I hadn't given that any thought. I don't know whether someone brought me—I can't remember whether I was given an address, I really can't remember that, the sequence there.

Q: Now, you described the mimeographed material which you gave, can you recall the

The Sylvia Franklin Dossier, published by the International Committee of the Fourth International in 1977

contents of the material that you typed?

A: Well, I remember I used to just type up—it was mostly during the faction fights in the party and political committee meetings, who was fighting with who, and then if there was correspondence from Leon Trotsky that I saw, I would try to remember what was in the letters and write that all out, who's going with who and that kind of thing, personal things like that, I remember, how much money they had—I knew, you know, bank balances and stuff like that.[70]

Callen and the GPU had access to everything: international correspondence, internal discussion papers from Trotskyist movements worldwide, all of Cannon's correspondence, and personal information about the membership.

---

70. Ibid., p. 29.

The release of the grand jury transcripts exploded the cover-up of the GPU's penetration of the SWP, and completely vindicated the investigation conducted by the International Committee.

But Judge Pfaelzer, guided by a desire to prevent Gelfand from exposing the depth of the FBI's involvement in the SWP, denied his requests that she release information about specific agents operating in the party.

Pfaelzer ruled against Gelfand by conjuring up a clearly unattainable level of proof.

Pfaelzer asserted that Gelfand could not prove his case by a "preponderance of evidence" if there were other explanations—no matter how implausible—for the SWP defendants' actions. The judge acknowledged that Gelfand's conclusion that the SWP leaders were agents "might be a permissible inference to be drawn, but you can't prevail by a preponderance of the evidence on that because it's equally likely that they just sat there without investigating because they had blind faith. *You can't win on a preponderance of the evidence based solely on the fact that the charges were true.*" (Emphasis added).[71]

"*Dossier of a Double Agent: The Lies of Joseph Hansen,*" part of the Security and the Fourth International investigation

In a further exchange with Gelfand's attorney, Pfaelzer said:

> Let us assume that you prove that every single thing that Mr. Gelfand said is true and that there is no doubt that Hansen was working with the FBI and may indeed have been an agent of the FBI at some point, and that Sylvia Caldwell was an agent of the GPU, and that indeed his suspicions were well founded and

---

71. *The Gelfand Case*, vol. 2, p. 569.

they made a mistake, the party made a mistake in believing the contents of *Healy's Big Lie*.

Now, let's say that is all proved, what permissible inference may be drawn from that if that is all you have?

Burton said, "Your Honor, it can't be examined out of context."

To which Pfaelzer responded, "Oh, no. It can be examined out of context."[72]

This reasoning does not stand up to basic legal analysis. As all first year law students know, the "preponderance of evidence" standard only requires a civil plaintiff show there is a greater than 50 percent chance that the evidence presented proves the claim, not that all other potential inferences have been disproven. Furthermore, circumstantial evidence is always evaluated in context and frequently incriminating evidence can lose its meaning when viewed in isolation.

As the Workers League correctly noted, "The central pillar of the SWP's defense—that Gelfand had been propagating a 'slander campaign' manufactured by the International Committee—was utterly shattered. The transcripts' release completed the destruction of the defendants' credibility."[73]

Joseph Hansen and the Control Commission

Joseph Hansen, who had died in 1979, could not be deposed or questioned during the Gelfand Case. To the end, Hansen actively defended Callen, however, having organized an international campaign to slander those who raised questions about what was ultimately proven to be the truth: she was an agent of the GPU.

Why did Hansen, and the SWP after his death, go to such lengths to defend Callen? Why did they not simply admit, even before the release of the grand jury transcripts, that James P. Cannon's secretary had been an agent of the GPU from 1939 to 1947? By 1975, when the International Committee initiated its investigation into *Security and the Fourth International*, nearly thirty years had passed since Callen left the SWP.

The obvious question is: Why did Hansen and Barnes cling so desperately to the transparent lie that Callen had been an "exemplary" comrade? Would it

---

72. Ibid., pp. 568–569.
73. Ibid., p. 571.

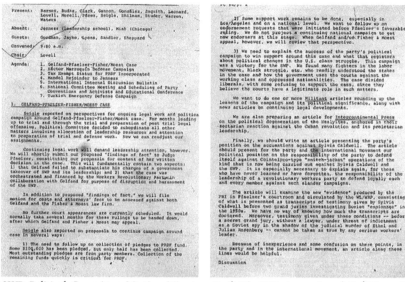

SWP Political Committee Meeting Minutes, April 16, 1983, pages 1 and 2 (Wisconsin Historical Society (See Appendix B, pp. 167–168)

not have been easier for Hansen to admit that the SWP had been duped by Callen's claims of innocence, and that the 1947 Control Commission's investigation had been inadequate?

The only answer is that the activities of Callen and Hansen were too closely intertwined. Hansen was compelled to lie about Sylvia Callen because—as a document obtained by Gelfand's attorneys near the conclusion of the litigation proved—he was shielding his own role as an agent inside the SWP.

Late in the litigation, Judge Pfaelzer compelled the SWP to turn over a letter sent to Hansen by his close friend, Vaughn T. "Irish" O'Brien.

In this letter, dated June 8, 1976, O'Brien recalled an encounter in the late 1940s or early 1950s—the general time frame of the Control Commission and the publication of Budenz's books—with Pearl Kluger, a former member of A.J. Muste's American Workers Party who knew Budenz personally. O'Brien wrote, "I had not seen Pearl for a considerable period of time, but she immediately said, 'Budenz says your friend Joe Hansen worked with the GPU.'"[74]

This extraordinary revelation—that the same man who had originally exposed Sylvia Callen had also identified Joseph Hansen as a GPU agent—was substantiated by the Socialist Workers Party. Just one month after the

---

74. Ibid., pp. 651–654.

conclusion of the Gelfand trial, in the April 15, 1983 edition of the *Militant*, SWP leader Larry Seigle wrote that Budenz "had fingered not just CP members, but also several SWP members, as Soviet agents. Among these were Joseph Hansen, a central leader of the SWP until his death in 1979, and Sylvia Caldwell, who had been a secretary in the SWP national office."[75]

It is evident that there were, in the immediate aftermath of the Gelfand trial, disagreements within the SWP leadership as to how to handle the evidence that incriminated Hansen as a GPU operative. Seigle's public acknowledgment of Budenz's exposure of both Caldwell *and* Hansen—thus confirming the allegations made by Gelfand—was evidently seen as a major political blunder.

Just one day after Seigle's article appeared in the *Militant*, the SWP leadership formulated a plan to reverse the damaging admission. The minutes from the SWP Political Committee meeting of April 16, 1983 show that the Barnes leadership conspired to denounce the grand jury transcripts as forgeries and double down on its defense of Callen-Caldwell:

> We should write an article presenting the party's position on the accusations against Sylvia Caldwell. The article should present for the party and the international movement our political position on the responsibility of the party to defend itself against Cointelpro-type "snitch-jacket" operations of the kind that is now being carried out against Sylvia Caldwell and the SWP. It is especially necessary to explain again, for those who have never learned or have forgotten, the responsibility of the leadership of a revolutionary workers party to defend loyally each and every member against such slander campaigns.
>
> The article will examine the new "evidence" presented by the FBI in Pfaelzer's courtroom and circulated by the WL/WRP, consisting of what is presented as transcripts of testimony given by Sylvia Caldwell before two grand juries investigating Soviet "espionage" in the 1950s. We have no way of knowing how much the transcripts are doctored. Moreover, testimony given under these conditions—before a secret grand jury, without a lawyer, under threat of indictment as a Soviet spy in the

---

75. The *Militant*, April 15, 1983. Available: http://www.themilitant.com/1983/4713/MIL4713.pdf.

shadow of the judicial murder of Ethel and Julius Rosenberg—
cannot be taken as true by any serious workers' leader.[76]

The minutes also reveal that the publication of the grand jury transcripts, exposing the cover-up of Sylvia Franklin, had produced widespread anxiety within the SWP membership and among its international allies.

Because of inexperience and some confusion on these points, in the party and in the international movement, an article along these lines would be helpful.[77]

On August 5, 1983, the *Militant* published a report that had been given by Jack Barnes in May, weeks after the PC meeting, to the SWP's National Committee. Barnes resumed the defense of Callen-Caldwell:

Another thing that happened at the trial needs to be emphasized. And that is what the government and the WL-WRP did concerning our comrade Sylvia Caldwell, whom they accuse of having been an agent of the Soviet secret police during the years when she was a member of our party, from the mid 1930s to the late-1940s. As we know, Sylvia was vilified by the FBI disrupter and stool pigeon, Louis Budenz. She was hounded by the FBI throughout the years of the witch-hunt. She was hauled before the federal grand juries investigating Soviet "espionage" during the 1950s, like the one that indicted the Rosenbergs. And she has now had the WL-WRP continuing the effort as a means of furthering their disruption operation against our movement, here and internationally.[78]

This tirade was a lie from beginning to end. If "our comrade Sylvia Caldwell" had been, as Barnes claimed, the subject of vicious persecution throughout the 1950s, why had the SWP failed to mount a public campaign in her defense? Why was there not a word written in the *Militant* about "comrade Sylvia" being "hauled before federal grand juries investigating Soviet 'espionage' during the

---

76. SWP PC meeting minutes April 16, 1983.
77. Ibid.
78. The *Militant*, August 5, 1983, p. 13. Available: http://www.themilitant.com/1983/4729/MIL4729.pdf

1950's, like the one that indicted the Rosenbergs"? Why had the SWP and the *Militant* not denounced publicly the listing of Sylvia Callen as a GPU co-conspirator in the 1960 federal indictment of Robert Soblen?

Barnes went on to imply that the 1958 transcript was a forgery, referring to it as "what the FBI claims is a transcript of her testimony before a grand jury in 1958." He continued:

> This is supposed to be the perfect frame—an official transcript, in which the woman under oath herself says that she did the things she was accused of doing. (I leave aside the fact that nowhere in the transcript is there any mention of the Soviet secret police, or any activity by Sylvia on their behalf. All it quotes her as saying is that she was gathering information for the Communist Party [CP]. It is revealing that, for the WL-WRP as for the FBI, being a member of the CP and being a Soviet espionage agent are the same thing.)[79]

The intense involvement of the Communist Party in the operations of the GPU—and especially in the penetration of the Fourth International and the SWP and in the organization of Trotsky's assassination—is an indisputable and massively documented historical fact. Budenz's own writings and testimony had made very clear that he, and those whom he recruited for anti-Trotskyist espionage activity, had been working for the GPU. Barnes' claim that "Sylvia's" admission that "she was gathering information for the Communist Party" does not prove that she was acting on behalf of the GPU testifies as much to his desperation as to his unscrupulous dishonesty. The reasons for Barnes' desperation are to be found in the evidence uncovered in the course of the Gelfand case and the *Security and the Fourth International* investigation.

The significance of the O'Brien letter, and Seigle's and Barnes' statements about the release of the 1958 transcript was summed up by David North in an article titled "Barnes Still Defends Sylvia Franklin," which appeared in the *Bulletin*, the newspaper of the Workers League, on September 9, 1983. North wrote:

> The transcripts showed that the facts presented by Louis F. Budenz, ex-editor of the Stalinist *Daily Worker*, in his November

---

79. Ibid..

Members of "The 18" SWP members jailed for sedition during World War Two

1950 affidavit exposing Franklin, were absolutely true. Franklin explicitly admitted in her testimony that she had been a member of the Communist Party and that she had been recruited by Louis Budenz to work as a spy inside the SWP.

These transcripts shattered the decades-old coverup of the true role of Franklin inside the SWP. The countless lies of Joseph Hansen, Barnes, and their accomplice George Novack in her defense ("an exemplary comrade," "a warm human being," "Budenz' foul slander," "Healy's Big Lie," etc.) were exposed once and for all.

Furthermore, other evidence introduced at trial established the full significance of the Franklin coverup. Budenz, it emerged, had also identified Hansen as a GPU agent at about the same time he had identified Franklin. This fact was contained in a letter written on June 8, 1976 to Joseph Hansen by his close friend, Vaughn T. O'Brien.[80]

After quoting Seigle's April 15, 1983 article noting that Budenz had also fingered "several SWP members," including Joseph Hansen, as GPU agents, North continued:

---

80. *Barnes Still Defends Sylvia Franklin*, p. 2.

Although he publicly exposed Franklin, Budenz never published what he knew about the GPU activities of Hansen. This was because he was instructed not to do so by the FBI. It was protecting its highly-prized agent inside the SWP, Joseph Hansen—who, as other evidence established, had sought and obtained a covert relationship with the FBI in 1940.[81]

It was essential, from the standpoint of the SWP's cover-up, that Budenz, as a source of the claim that both Callen and Hansen were agents, be labeled a "slanderer," "stoolpigeon," and "perjurer." Moreover, if Hansen and the SWP were to admit that Callen was an agent, it would lend legitimacy to Shachtman and Glotzer's 1947 source. This source not only warned about Callen, but also said, in the words of Cannon, that "the FBI has an agent in our party, high in the leadership." Cannon said Shachtman's Workers Party had warned the SWP of the FBI agent "for years."

The *Security and the Fourth International* investigation uncovered documents revealing that Hansen met secretly with the State Department in the aftermath of Trotsky's assassination. At these meetings, Hansen admitted to having a relationship with the GPU at the same exact time the Stalinists were infiltrating the SWP with agents like Franklin. He asked for, and received, information for follow-up meetings with the FBI in New York City. None of these facts were known to the National Committee of the SWP until the International Committee published them.

While Hansen's role as an agent is clear, the full details of his operations with the GPU and US agencies are not yet known. There were multiple sides to his motivation for initiating contact with the State Department and FBI. He feared that if US officials knew he had been in contact with the GPU, he would need an alibi, which he provided to the agents with whom he met after Trotsky's assassination. He also hoped to deflect attention from his past connections to the GPU in the investigations into Trotsky's assassination.

Hansen began working for the FBI, handing over to them information about the SWP's internal investigation into the assassination, as well as providing the US government a copy of the "W Memorandum," a list of names of GPU agents the SWP had received from ex-Communist Party member Whittaker Chambers.

---

81. Ibid.

In exchange for this and other internal party information, Hansen was able to avoid prosecution when, in 1941, the Justice Department, at the behest of the FBI, prosecuted twenty-nine members of the SWP with sedition and conspiracy to overthrow the government in the Minneapolis Smith Act Trial. As detailed in the review of Donna Haverty-Stacke's book *Trotskyists on Trial*, Hansen's absence from the list of defendants was otherwise inexplicable on account of his role as Trotsky's secretary in Mexico City from 1939 to 1940.

While the documents published by the ICFI showed Hansen's relationship with the FBI began in 1940, they do not indicate that this relationship ever came to an end.

The SWP had the opportunity to uncover the truth about Callen and Hansen. If the 1947 SWP Control Commission had made a real effort to investigate the claims about FBI and GPU infiltration by Shachtman and Glotzer's source, which followed the Budenz revelations, they would have exposed the agents who did untold damage to the SWP over the course of the next decades, including Hansen himself. In the course of the SWP's suit against the FBI over COINTELPRO, the government was forced to admit that it had infiltrated the SWP with hundreds of agents, comprising a substantial portion of the party membership. Soviet spy logs and cables, acquired by the US Army Signals Intelligence through the VENONA program, which were published in the mid-1990s, explicitly reference Callen—codename "Satyr"—as a Soviet agent.

Instead, the Control Commission let the matter pass and swore those present to secrecy. Callen was allowed to leave the movement without any public statement from the party explaining her sudden departure. The SWP dropped all coverage of Louis Budenz's revelations at precisely the time the government was acting on the SWP's prior demand that Budenz be interviewed by a grand jury. When Budenz published his second book in 1950, *Men Without Faces*, the SWP worked with Callen herself, who dictated to Farrell Dobbs how the SWP should respond to Budenz's allegations.

Hansen maneuvered to protect Callen, as evidenced by his exchanges with Isaac Don Levine in 1958 and Gerry Healy in 1960. The SWP failed to report on the 1960 Robert Soblen trial and the testimony of Jack Soble, which further identified Callen as an agent. Cannon, in his 1966 letter to Reba Hansen, also gave a false portrayal of the 1947 Control Commission, indicating that it investigated the matter and allowed Callen to "continue with her work."

As a result, Hansen remained at his leadership post, with access to information about the world movement's activities and membership. Throughout the 1960s and 1970s, Hansen became the dominant political figure in the SWP, engineering its political break with the International Committee in 1963 and its reunification with the pro-Stalinist United Secretariat of Michel Pablo. Hansen also oversaw the recruitment of Jack Barnes and a group of twelve students from Carleton College, a rural private college in Minnesota, and helped orchestrate their elevation into the leadership of the party.

The ICFI's *Security and the Fourth International* investigation was an enormous undertaking and a milestone in the history of the Trotskyist movement. The ICFI conducted this struggle under conditions where the Stalinist bureaucracy and Pabloite apparatus wielded considerable influence over the labor movement and sought to blackguard and isolate the ICFI.

Despite these unfavorable circumstances, the ICFI fought to expose the crimes of the Stalinist bureaucracy in orchestrating the murder of Trotsky and the infiltration of the Trotskyist movement.

To the contemporary reader, it might seem difficult to understand the bitterness of the denunciations that were hurled against the ICFI for undertaking this investigation. Opposition to the *Security and the Fourth International* investigation from the various Pabloite and Stalinist organizations had two central motivations. First, the state agents inside the SWP and the international Pabloite organizations were determined to block their own exposure through the ICFI's investigation. Second, and most fundamentally, *Security and the Fourth International's* exposure of the counterrevolutionary history and role of Stalinism cut across the political agenda of the Pabloites and their Stalinist allies.

But, over the past forty years, the publication of new evidence has substantiated the ICFI's allegations as fact. Even today, many who cite the information made public through *Security and the Fourth International* do so without acknowledging the investigation itself or the ICFI's role.

The lies to defend Hansen and to slander the *Security and the Fourth International* investigation continue to the present. The ex-Pabloite, St. Mary's professor Susan Weissman, for example, called the investigation "a bizarre, sectarian smear campaign against Joseph Hansen." When challenged to retract her slanders in a November 10, 2015 open letter by David North, Weissman hid behind a veil of dishonest silence.

To honest historians, as well as workers and youth coming into struggle with the capitalist system, the investigation is an invaluable source for understanding the nature of the state, the counterrevolutionary character of the Stalinist bureaucracy and the necessity of protecting the revolutionary movement from agents of the government. The historical significance of *Security and the Fourth International* endures.

Appendix A

An Open Letter from David North to Susan Weissman

Security and the Fourth International, the Gelfand Case and the Deposition of Mark Zborowski

Dear Ms. Weissman,

This letter is a formal request that you fully, unequivocally and publicly retract the false statements maligning the International Committee of the Fourth International and the attorney Alan Gelfand with which you conclude the second part of your article, "Mark 'Etienne' Zborowski: Portrait of Deception," published this past summer in *Critique: Journal of Socialist Theory*.[1]

The statements to which we object appear beneath the heading "Postscripts." They are not merely factual misstatements, regrettable but unintentional, but consist of a series of willful distortions of fact and outright lies.

You have resorted to slander in order to discredit the investigation, initiated by the International Committee in 1975, into the penetration of the Fourth International by agents of the Soviet secret police, the GPU-NKVD. This investigation, known as *Security and the Fourth International,* remains to this day the most detailed exposition of the role played by Stalinist agents in the assassination of key figures in the Fourth International and, finally, of Trotsky himself. Indeed, the two articles that you have published in

1. Volume 39, No. 4, pp. 583–609 ; Volume 43, No. 2, pp. 189–209

Published on the World Socialist Web Site November 10, 2015

Critique—to the extent that they are grounded in a factual record—draw heavily, though without proper attribution, upon the research conducted by the International Committee 40 years ago. Your failure to forthrightly acknowledge your own use of the pioneering work of *Security and the Fourth International* constitutes intellectual plagiarism.

Your attack on Alan Gelfand and the lawsuit that he initiated against the Socialist Workers Party in 1979 is particularly reprehensible, inasmuch as his efforts led to the release of documents—such as the grand jury transcripts of GPU agent Sylvia Caldwell (aka Callen, Franklin and Doxsee)—that are widely cited by historians in works dealing with the criminal activities of the Soviet secret police.[2]

The dishonest and malicious character of your "postscript" is made all too clear by the fact that you have concealed the political motivations underlying your attack on the International Committee and Gelfand. Following the postscript, there is a final "Disclosure Statement," which reads, "No potential conflict of interest was reported by the author."[3] You are guilty, Ms. Weissman, of filing a false disclosure statement for the purpose of intentionally withholding important information from the readers of *Critique*.

Your extreme hostility to the *Security and the Fourth International* investigation is inextricably linked to your political affiliations. You have been active in Pabloite politics for 40 years, and have over all these decades opposed the International Committee's investigation into GPU penetration of the Fourth International and the circumstances surrounding Trotsky's assassination. You are a member of the Solidarity organization, formed largely by ex-members of the SWP, and joined the editorial board of its journal, *Against the Current*, in 1986. Many of your closest political associates are on record denouncing *Security and the Fourth International* as a "slander campaign." You, Ms. Weissman, never objected to the Socialist Workers Party's praise of Sylvia Caldwell as an "exemplary comrade," and you agree with the SWP's characterization of efforts to uncover and expose state infiltration of the Fourth International as "agent-baiting" and "paranoia."

You have privately spread lies about the research of the International Committee, describing *Security and the Fourth International* as "garbage" in a 1996 letter to the late Albert Glotzer, a founding member of the Socialist

---

2. See, for example, *The Venona Secrets: Exposing Soviet Espionage and American Traitors*, by Herbert Romerstein and Èric Breindel; and *Spies: The Rise and Fall of the KGB in America*, by Harvey Klehr, John Earl Haynes, and Alexander Vassiliev.

3. *Critique*, vol. 43, p. 209.

Workers Party. Nothing troubles you more than signs that *Security and the Fourth International* is being read by mainstream historians. Referring to a work written by a noted Soviet historian, you wrote to Glotzer: "What is very disturbing in the Volkogonov book, in the section on the Trotsky assassination, is that he bases himself not only on Sudoplatov, but even worse on the American Healyites (or 'Northites') from the 'Gelfand Case.'"[4] Sudoplatov, as you know, was a notorious KGB killer, who played a central role in planning Trotsky's assassination. That you consider "the Northites" "even worse" than a GPU-NKVD murderer exposes not only the depth of your subjective hatred of the International Committee, but also the political outlook that underlies your Zborowski project.

You fail to tell your readers that you supported the expulsion of Alan Gelfand from the Socialist Workers Party for demanding that the SWP renounce its defense of Sylvia Caldwell and that Joseph Hansen, a central leader of the organization, reply to documents published by the International Committee exposing his own secret dealings with the GPU and the US Federal Bureau of Investigation in the 1930s and 1940s. Above all, Ms. Weissman, you still endorse and continue to cover up the efforts of the SWP in 1981–1983 to obstruct and suppress Alan Gelfand's attempts to compel Sylvia Caldwell and Mark Zborowski to testify under oath about their murderous activities inside the Trotskyist movement.

Your filing of a false disclosure statement not only discredits your attack on the ICFI and Alan Gelfand. It also raises serious questions about the nature and purpose of your research into the activities of Mark Zborowski as an agent inside the Fourth International. In light of the dishonest character of your "postscript," the integrity of your Zborowski project is highly suspect. The subtitle of your article on Zborowski, "Portrait of Deception," could justly serve as a description of your own efforts.

Let us turn to a detailed examination of your postscript. The entire text of the concluding paragraph reads:

> In 1979, the Workers League, US co-thinkers of Gerry Healy's British Socialist Labor League and the International Committee of the Fourth International, discovered where Zborowski lived in San Francisco and picketed his house. That organisation initiated a bizarre, sectarian smear campaign against Joseph Hansen, a

---

4. Letter to Albert Glotzer, December 13, 1996.

leader of the US Socialist Workers Party, who was one of Trotsky's
secretaries at Calle Viena in Coyoacán, Mexico. In the notorious
Gelfand case, named for the lawyer Alan Gelfand who filed the
lawsuit against the SWP and Joseph Hansen, the Workers League
charged that key leaders of the SWP were FBI agents and that
Joseph Hansen was an agent of the FBI and the GPU. The case was
both frivolous and groundless, but provided headlines and ink for
Healy's organisations. The relevance for this work is that Gelfand
succeeded in deposing Zborowski in April 1982. Zborowski ran
rings around Gelfand and his attorney, refusing to answer anything more than the year and place of his birth and whether he
had any siblings. The case was eventually dismissed. Once again,
Zborowski proved himself a master at revealing nothing, taking
the fifth and making fools of his questioners.[5]

Virtually every sentence in this paragraph consists of factual inaccuracies,
misleading presentations of the underlying events and issues, half-truths and
outright lies.

**1. "In 1979, the Workers League, US co-thinkers of Gerry Healy's British
Socialist Labor [sic] League and the International Committee of the
Fourth International, discovered where Zborowski lived in San Francisco
and picketed his house."**

You are incapable, as a result of carelessness and malice, of getting even the
most elementary facts correct. The Workers League discovered Zborowski's
address in San Francisco not in 1979, but in 1975. This four-year discrepancy
distorts the narrative of events that led to Alan Gelfand's decision to file a lawsuit against the Socialist Workers Party, which occurred after his expulsion in
January 1979. Also, the Workers League did not picket Zborowski's house.
Acting on behalf of the International Committee, I photographed Zborowski
and his wife outside their apartment in August 1975. These photos were
included in *How the GPU Murdered Trotsky*, the initial interim report of the
Security and the Fourth International investigation.

**2. "That organisation initiated a bizarre, sectarian smear campaign against
Joseph Hansen, a leader of the US Socialist Workers Party, who was one of
Trotsky's secretaries at Calle Viena in Coyoacán, Mexico."**

---

5. *Critique*, p. 209.

Your description of *Security and the Fourth International* as a "bizarre sectarian smear campaign against Joseph Hansen" is a defamatory falsification of the origins and nature of the accusations leveled by the International Committee against Joseph Hansen. *How the GPU Murdered Trotsky* was serialized in the press of the International Committee in August-September 1975. This meticulously researched historical narrative provided, for the first time in the history of the Fourth International, a detailed account of the conspiracy against Trotsky's life. With the exception of a single report written in the immediate aftermath of Trotsky's assassination, the Socialist Workers Party made no effort to uncover and expose the GPU-NKVD network that infiltrated the Fourth International and organized Trotsky's murder. Basing itself on official US government documents, the transcripts of Congressional hearings, and the testimony of Soviet agents who were placed on trial in the 1950s, the International Committee reconstructed the vast network of GPU agents—in Paris, New York and Mexico—involved in the plot to murder Trotsky and destroy the Fourth International.

How the GPU Murdered Trotsky examined the origins of the GPU conspiracy against the international Trotskyist movement. It reviewed the activities of the Sobolevicius brothers (aka Senin and Well) and Mark Zborowski ("Etienne") in Europe. The information uncovered by the International Committee also raised disturbing questions about Lola Dallin (aka Estrine), Zborowski's self-described "Siamese Twin," who protected him unrelentingly, over a period of nearly 20 years, from the threat of exposure and, thereby, facilitated his crimes. The International Committee reviewed the manner in which Ramon Mercader (aka Frank Jacson) was successfully insinuated into the milieu of the Fourth International and initiated the personal relationship with SWP member Sylvia Ageloff that eventually gave the future assassin direct access to Trotsky.

How the GPU Murdered Trotsky dealt also with the network of GPU agents who penetrated the Trotskyist movement within the United States, including Thomas Black, Floyd Cleveland Miller and Sylvia Caldwell, who functioned as SWP founder James P. Cannon's personal secretary between 1938 and 1947. *How the GPU Murdered Trotsky* uncovered information about Robert Sheldon Harte—the American guard who opened the gates of the Coyoacán villa to the Stalinist machine gun squad that unsuccessfully attempted to assassinate Trotsky on May 24, 1940—which strongly suggested he had been a Stalinist agent.

The International Committee also unearthed US government documents that revealed for the first time that Joseph Hansen initiated, just 10 days after Trotsky's assassination, a series of secret meetings, totally unbeknownst to the Socialist Workers Party, with a representative of the FBI in the American Embassy in Mexico City. At the first meeting, Hansen informed FBI agent Robert McGregor that "when in New York in 1938 he was himself approached by an agent of the GPU and asked to desert the Fourth International and join the Third." Claiming to act with Trotsky's approval, Hansen told the FBI that for three months he "had relations with a man who merely identified himself as 'John,' and did not otherwise reveal his true identity."[6]

Confronted with this previously unknown information, the International Committee demanded that Hansen provide an explanation of his contacts with the FBI and relationship with the GPU.

Hansen's response to *How the GPU Murdered Trotsky* was nothing less than astonishing. He simply dismissed the documents that memorialized his meeting with the FBI as a "geyser of mud,"[7] without providing any evidence that this and subsequent meetings with representatives of the "American Gestapo"—as the SWP publicly labeled the FBI in 1940—were authorized by the SWP leadership. Nor did Hansen provide any credible explanation for his meetings with the GPU agent "John."

At the same time, Hansen issued a deceitful defense of Cannon's personal secretary. "Sylvia Caldwell (that was her party name)," he wrote in a lengthy statement published in the November 24, 1975 issue of the SWP's *Intercontinental Press*, "worked very hard in her rather difficult assignment of managing the national office of the Socialist Workers party, which included helping Cannon in a secretarial capacity. In fact all the comrades who shared these often irksome chores with her regarded her as exemplary. They burned as much as she did over the foul slander spread by Budenz."[8]

Louis Budenz, as you well know, Ms. Weissman, was the one-time Stalinist editor of the *Daily Worker*, who was an agent of the GPU in the United States and played a central role in the conspiracy to murder Trotsky. After defecting from the Communist Party, Budenz went over to the FBI and began identifying agents whom the GPU had sent into the Trotskyist Socialist Workers Party. One of those agents was Sylvia Caldwell, who disappeared from the

---

6. *How the GPU Murdered Trotsky* (London: New Park, 1981), pp. 217–218.
7. *Healy's Big Lie: The Slander Campaign Against Joseph Hansen, George Novack, and the Fourth International* (New York: National Education Department, 1976), p. 13.
8. Ibid., p. 9.

SWP in 1947, shortly after Budenz had exposed her. In 1960, Sylvia Callen (Caldwell's maiden name) was named an unindicted co-conspirator in the trial of Robert Soblen for espionage. Robert Soblen—I should not need to inform you—was one of the aforementioned Sobolevicius brothers who had first infiltrated the Trotskyist movement in the early 1930s. His brother, Jack Soble, who was found guilty of espionage in the 1950s, had during his trial also identified Cannon's secretary as a GPU agent.

Hansen also denounced the questions raised by the ICFI about Robert Sheldon Harte as "particularly vile," declaring: "The odor of the old GPU slanders against Harte, we see, still persists in the headquarters of the Workers Revolutionary party."[9]

Following the publication of *How the GPU Murdered Trotsky*, the International Committee uncovered more government documents relating to Hansen's contacts with the FBI.[10] They revealed that Hansen's relationship with the FBI was intense and open-ended. It involved a one-sided exchange of information, from Hansen to the FBI. He provided information identifying various US citizens as GPU agents. He handed over to the FBI a secret memorandum, authored by Whittaker Chambers (another defector from the GPU) that implicated SWP member Sylvia Ageloff in Trotsky's murder. It stated: "Cannot believe innocence of Ageloff girls. Only a moron could live with GPU agent and not become cognizant." Whether or not Chambers' assessment was justified remains a matter of legitimate debate. But at the time Hansen transmitted this document to the FBI, which incriminated a party comrade, the public position of the Socialist Workers Party was that Sylvia Ageloff was an innocent victim of the assassin's criminal duplicity.

FBI director J. Edgar Hoover closely monitored Hansen's meetings with the FBI and ordered that no information relating to the FBI's investigation of Trotsky's murder be given to him.

Finally, before returning to New York from Mexico, Joseph Hansen asked that he be provided with a confidential FBI contact "to whom confidential information could be imparted with impunity."[11]

3. "In the notorious Gelfand case, named for the lawyer Alan Gelfand who filed the lawsuit against the SWP and Joseph Hansen, the Workers League

---

9. Ibid., pp. 9–11.

10. The texts of these documents are reprinted in *The Gelfand Case*, Volume 1, (New York: Labor Publications, 1985), pp. 7–30.

11. Ibid., p. 21.

charged that key leaders of the SWP were FBI agents and that Joseph Hansen was an agent of the FBI and the GPU. The case was both frivolous and groundless, but provided headlines and ink for Healy's organisations."

There was nothing "frivolous and groundless"—let alone "notorious"—about the lawsuit initiated by Gelfand in July 1979. It was based on a massive body of evidence. Had the lawsuit been "frivolous and groundless," it would not have survived the three motions for summary judgment brought by the SWP. On July 12, 1982, Judge Marianna Pfaelzer denied summary judgment, acknowledging that Gelfand had met the legal test required to establish a triable issue of fact. Thus, the case went to trial. As a matter of law, this ruling meant that the Court found Gelfand's suit to be neither "frivolous" nor "groundless." It objectively demolished the official SWP claim, which you uphold to this day, that "Healy and his associates have not brought forward the slightest probative evidence, documents, or testimony to substantiate their libelous accusations against Hansen and Novack, the nominal targets of the attacks."[12]

For more than a year prior to his expulsion from the SWP in 1979 and the initiation of his lawsuit, Gelfand had attempted to obtain from national secretary Jack Barnes and other party leaders a factually grounded and coherent explanation of the incriminating documents published by the International Committee. No explanation was provided. Instead, he was referred to the SWP Education Bulletin entitled "Healy's Big Lie." Gelfand was told, falsely, that all the issues raised by the International Committee had been answered in this Bulletin. This Bulletin, as was apparent to anyone who took the time to read it carefully, answered nothing. You, Ms. Weissman, were apparently satisfied with the SWP's refusal to provide credible answers to evidence establishing that Sylvia Caldwell was an agent and that Joseph Hansen served as an FBI informer. But Gelfand was not.

In a letter to the SWP National Committee, dated March 26, 1978, Gelfand carefully reviewed the documents and related evidence uncovered by the International Committee. He presented the national committee with three questions:

> I. Was Sylvia Franklin, personal secretary to James P. Cannon, a GPU agent?
> II. Was Joseph Hansen authorized by the SWP to have personal contact with the GPU in 1938?

---

12. *Healy's Big Lie*, p. 63.

III. Was Joseph Hansen authorized by the SWP to meet with the FBI in 1940?[13]

Gelfand, a highly experienced public defense lawyer, included with each question a detailed review of the documentary evidence produced by the International Committee. In the concluding section of his letter, Gelfand wrote:

> I am confident that upon any objective reading of my letter one will conclude that Sylvia Franklin was a GPU agent and that Joseph Hansen's relationship with the GPU and FBI are at the minimum, highly questionable, and in need of an immediate and exhaustive examination.[14]

Gelfand ended his letter with two demands:

> 1. That Sylvia Franklin be repudiated as a GPU agent.
> 2. That Joseph Hansen be required to give a complete and full accounting of his involvement with the GPU and the FBI, and that he hand over to the Party any and all files, memos, manuscripts, letters or other correspondence in his possession or under his control.[15]

On April 7, 1978, Larry Seigle, writing on behalf of the SWP Political Committee, replied to Gelfand with the following warning:

> You have asked for our opinion about how you may proceed to press your charges against Joe Hansen. The answer to that question is simple. The Party cannot and will not allow agent-baiting within its ranks. Any further repetition by you of the Healyite slanders will not be tolerated.[16]

Seigle's letter made it clear that the SWP leadership was unable to answer and refute the evidence published by the International Committee, and that

---

13. *The Gelfand Case*, Volume 1, pp. 52–70.
14. Ibid., p. 69.
15. Ibid., p. 70.
16. Ibid., p. 74.

its only response to those who sought answers was to threaten them with expulsion from the SWP.

On December 18, 1978, Gelfand filed an *amicus curiae* (friend of the court) brief in federal court demanding that the US attorney general "disclose the names of all the informants in the SWP, both past and present..."[17] Just short of one month later, on January 11, 1979, the SWP Political Committee responded to this politically principled demand by expelling Alan Gelfand from the SWP. In a public statement issued by the SWP leadership in July 1979, Seigle wrote that Gelfand's "expulsion was overdue."[18]

You persist to this day in slandering Gelfand despite the fact that his questions about the infiltration of the Socialist Workers Party have been entirely vindicated.

Permit me to call your attention to certain indisputable facts:

First, the Venona Papers and documents obtained after the dissolution of the Soviet Union have confirmed that Robert Sheldon Harte—whom Hansen and his colleague George Novack had eulogized as an innocent victim of "Healy's Big Lie"—had been recruited by the GPU and was a participant in the May 24, 1940 attempt on Trotsky's life:

> KGB archival material brought to the West by Vasili Mitrokhin confirmed that Harte had collaborated with the attackers. A history of the KGB published in Russia in 1997 noted that Harte willingly opened the gate and left with the assailants, asserting that he had been recruited by the New York station and given the cover name "Cupid."[19]

Thus, the questions about Harte initially raised by the International Committee in *How the GPU Murdered Trotsky*—and for which it was viciously maligned by Hansen and Novack—were completely legitimate. There is, one must note, no reference to Sheldon Harte in your *Critique* articles.

Second, it has been established that Sylvia Caldwell was a GPU agent. Gelfand's lawsuit led to the release of her 1958 grand jury testimony in which

---

17. Ibid., p. 91.

18. Ibid., p. 103

19. Harvey Klehr, John Earl Haynes, Alexander Vassiliev: *Spies: The Rise and Fall of the KGB in America* (Kindle Locations 7502-7505). Kindle Edition.

she confessed her role as a Stalinist spy in the SWP. Even you have finally acknowledged that she was an agent. You write in the *Critique* article:

> Instead, Mike Cort, also known as Floyd Cleveland Miller, became the KGB's main agent in the SWP, along with Sylvia Callen, who served as James Cannon's secretary, a position that gave her access to internal documents and information about SWP activities. Sylvia's name in the Trotskyist movement was Caldwell, but she was also known by the last names of the men she married, first Zalmond Franklin (also an agent), then James Doxsee. Her cover name in the Venona traffic was Satyr. She regularly supplied her NKVD controller Jack Soble with typewritten reports about the factional struggles within the SWP, but continually asked to be released from the work because it made her nervous. Joseph Katz was put in charge of both Cort and Caldwell, under Soble's direction.[20]

The Venona papers—transcripts of decoded Soviet espionage reports that were released by the US government following the dissolution of the USSR— added little to the information about Doxsee that had already been uncovered years earlier by the *Security and the Fourth International* investigation and Alan Gelfand's lawsuit. I had located Caldwell in Wheaton, Illinois in May 1977 and established that her new married name was Sylvia Doxsee. In March 1983, at the very conclusion of the trial of the Gelfand case, Judge Marianna Pfaelzer released, over the bitter objections of the Socialist Workers Party, the transcripts of Doxsee's grand jury testimony. Pfaelzer's action clearly took the SWP attorney, not to mention SWP National Secretary Jack Barnes, by surprise. Less than one hour before the transcripts were released, Barnes reaffirmed his admiration for Sylvia Franklin. The following exchange between Gelfand's attorney and Barnes took place in open court on March 9, 1983:

> Q: Now, was it your opinion at the time you received [Gelfand's letter] that there was no evidence whatsoever to indicate that Sylvia Franklin was an agent of the GPU?
> A [Barnes]: All the evidence is just the opposite. Her whole comportment not only when she was in the movement but

---

20. "Portrait of Deception," Part 2, *Critique*, 2015, Volume 43, No. 1, p. 192.

everything that's happened since she left indicates that she is exactly what she was: a loyal, hard-working, and model member of our movement.

Q: That is still your opinion today?

A: Well, my opinion today is she is one of my heroes after the harassment and what she's been through in the last couple of years. I would even feel more strongly about her, her character, than I did then.[21]

Third, a document obtained by Gelfand in the course of the discovery process established that Louis Budenz, who had exposed Sylvia Caldwell, had also identified Joseph Hansen as a GPU agent. A private letter written on June 8, 1976 to Joseph Hansen by his friend, Vaughn T. O'Brien recalled the following significant event:

Some years ago, in the late '40s or early '50s, (I am hazy on the date but clearly recall the place—Second Avenue and Seventeenth Street in NYC)—I encountered Pearl Kluger on the street. Pearl had been a secretary in the office of the American Committee for the Defense of Leon Trotsky and was, I believe, originally associated with A.J. Muste and Louis Bundenz [sic] in the old American Workers Party. I had not seen Pearl for a considerable period of time, but she immediately said, "Budenz says your friend Joe Hansen worked with the GPU."[22]

O'Brien's letter revealed, at long last, why Hansen and the SWP had relentlessly defended Sylvia Caldwell as an "exemplary" comrade in the face of overwhelming evidence (even prior to the release of the 1958 grand jury transcripts and the Venona Papers) that she was a GPU-KGB spy; and why they had again and again denounced Budenz as a perjurer. Budenz had fingered not only Caldwell, but Hansen as well. For the SWP to accept Budenz' allegations against Caldwell as true would have raised inexorably the most serious questions about Hansen's role. Moreover, the fact that Budenz never publicly identified Hansen as an agent would have inevitably raised the suspicion that the FBI had vetoed his exposure because Hansen had been functioning as a high-level informer since 1940.

---

21. *The Gelfand Case*, Volume 2, p. 635.
22. Ibid., p. 651.

Five weeks after the conclusion of the Gelfand trial, in the April 15, 1983 edition of the *Militant*, the SWP leaders informed their members for the first time of what they had known for years: that Budenz had named "several SWP members as Soviet agents. Among these were Joseph Hansen, a central leader of the SWP until his death in 1979..." The word "several" indicates that the list of GPU agents inside the SWP included more names than those of Hansen and Caldwell. Despite this staggering public admission, which entirely vindicated the *Security and the Fourth International* investigation and the efforts of Alan Gelfand, the SWP leaders decided to persist in their defense of Caldwell. Just one day after the damning admission published in the *Militant*, Larry Seigle made the following proposal to the SWP Political Committee:

> Finally, we should write an article presenting the party's position on the accusations against Sylvia Caldwell. The article should present for the party and the international movement our political position on the responsibility of the party to defend itself against Cointelpro-type "snitch-jacket" operations of the kind that is now being carried out against Sylvia Caldwell and the SWP. It is especially necessary to explain again, for those who have never learned or have forgotten, the responsibility of the leadership of a revolutionary workers party to defend loyally each and every member against such slander campaigns.[23]

The political committee minutes record that a motion "To approve the approach outlined by Seigle for the Sylvia Caldwell article" passed unanimously. This "approach" was realized in a report given by Jack Barnes to the national committee of the SWP in May 1983, which was published in the *Militant* on August 5, 1983. Barnes again embraced Caldwell as a "comrade." He told the national committee:

> As we know, Sylvia was vilified by the FBI disrupter and stool pigeon, Louis Budenz. She was hounded by the FBI throughout the years of the witch-hunt. She was hauled before federal grand juries investigating Soviet "espionage" during the 1950s, like the one that indicted the Rosenbergs. And she has now

---

23. SWP Political Committee Meeting No. 8, April 16, 1983.

had the WL-WRP continuing the effort as a means of furthering their disruption operation against our movement, here and
internationally.

Barnes went on to claim that the grand jury transcripts had been forged.
"This is supposed to be the perfect frame—an official transcript, in which the
woman under oath herself says that she did things she was accused of doing."[24]
Barnes' preposterous and desperate claims were accepted without objection
by the national committee.

**4. "The relevance for this work is that Gelfand succeeded in deposing
Zborowski in April 1982. Zborowski ran rings around Gelfand and his
attorney, refusing to answer anything more than the year and place of his
birth and whether he had any siblings. The case was eventually dismissed.
Once again, Zborowski proved himself a master at revealing nothing, taking the fifth and making fools of his questioners."**

Everything in the above-quoted passage is a distortion and falsification of
the legal record. Zborowski ran circles around no one. This is clearly shown
by the legal record surrounding Gelfand's efforts to depose Zborowski. On
February 1, 1982, Judge Pfaelzer granted Gelfand 90 days of discovery, during which time he would be allowed to depose witnesses to obtain information relevant to his case. Gelfand's attorneys proceeded to issue a subpoena to
Zborowski. The SWP immediately petitioned the court to impose a protec-
tive order blocking Zborowski's deposition. In his own deposition, in March
1982, Jack Barnes presented an extraordinary justification of the SWP's intervention in defense of Zborowski:

> Q: Is it your job to protect GPU agents?
> A [Barnes]: It is my job to protect the rights of American citi-
> zens by fighting and by working through the movement and
> defending the rights of our party, when they come under attack.
> Q: Are the rights of your party coming under attack when inves-
> tigations are conducted, within the confines of the law, into the
> activities of the GPU within your movement?
> A: When individuals are harassed by organizations whose sole
> purpose is to harass them their rights are affected. You referred

---

24. The *Militant*, August 5, 1983, p. 13. Available: http://www.themilitant.com/1983/4729/
MIL4729.pdf#page=10&view=fitH

to Mr. Zborowski earlier. He is a person who stated, under oath, associations with agencies alien to our movement. Even Mr. Zborowski has the same rights as any other citizen in this country.[25]

The issue was not whether Zborowski had rights, but whether he should be compelled to give testimony, in a lawful deposition, relating to his role as a Stalinist agent. In response to the SWP's efforts to block the deposition, Gelfand's attorneys submitted a brief, dated March 12, 1982, explaining the significance of Zborowski's testimony.

> Mr. Zborowski's deposition will shed valuable light on the nature of GPU activity in the American Trotskyist movement. He will be questioned as to the names of his collaborators inside that movement and as to his own activities inside the SWP. Given Mr. Zborowski's career within the Fourth International, it is clear that he can shed critical light on the activities of GPU agents and their modus operandi, an issue of great importance in evaluating the present-day activities of the SWP defendants. The importance of Mr. Zborowski's deposition is clear, and considering the historical record of his espionage within the Trotskyist movement, it is indeed odd that the SWP defendants have sought a protective order on his behalf.[26]

Judge Pfaelzer rejected the SWP's attempt to stop Zborowski's deposition, which then went forward on Thursday, April 15, 1982. At long last, this murderer was to be questioned by an attorney representing the Trotskyist movement. Zborowski had played a central role in 1) the July 1937 kidnapping-murder of Erwin Wolf, a key secretary of Leon Trotsky; 2) the September 1937 assassination of Ignatz Reiss, who had defected from the GPU and declared his support for the Fourth International; 3) the February 1938 assassination of Trotsky's son, Leon Sedov; and 4) the July 1938 kidnapping-murder of Rudolf Klement, the secretary of the Fourth International.

Zborowski's deposition was an event that should have been celebrated by every socialist. But for the Socialist Workers Party, which had tried to quash

---

25. *The Gelfand Case*, Volume 2, p. 422.
26. *The Gelfand Case*, Volume 1, pp. 152–153.

the deposition, it was a threat. Attorney James Larson represented Mark Zborowski. In the fight to stop the questioning of Zborowski, Larson worked closely with attorneys for the SWP. The US government was intensely interested in this deposition. An attorney for the government, Linda Cromwell, attended the deposition, representing CIA Director William Casey, FBI Director William Webster, and Attorney General William French Smith. John Burton, the attorney representing Alan Gelfand, questioned Zborowski.

After answering questions relating to his personal identity, Zborowski was asked when he had left Russia. He replied: "Upon the advice of my attorney, I decline to answer that question on the grounds that the answer may tend to incriminate me in violation of my state and federal privileges against self-incrimination." He asserted this privilege in response to all further questions from Burton, including the following critical question:

> Q: If I asked you questions relating to the circumstances of your entry into the United States during December of 1941, would your answer be the same?
> A [Zborowski]: Yes.

As you know, Ms. Weissman, Zborowski was able to escape pro-fascist Vichy France and enter the United States due to the extraordinary efforts made on his behalf by Lola Dallin and George Novack. An answer by Zborowski to this question would have contributed to clarifying the nature of his relationship with Dallin. Was she working with him as a collaborator in his GPU activities? Was George Novack part of a network of Stalinist sympathizers and operatives inside the SWP?

Burton pressed on with his interrogation of Zborowski, asking him if he would continue to assert the Fifth Amendment privilege against self-incrimination.

> Q: If I asked you questions relating to any activities you may have engaged in on behalf of the Soviet secret police within the Trotskyist movement and within the Socialist Workers Party in the United States from the time that you entered the United States through the years 1954 and 1955, would your answers be the same?
> A: Yes.
> Q: If I asked you questions relating to personal knowledge or hearsay knowledge that you might have of the international

apparatus of the Soviet secret police within the Trotskyist movement from 1930 to the present time, would your answer be the same?

A: Yes.[27]

Why do you describe Zborowski's invocation, on advice of counsel, of the Fifth Amendment privilege against self-incrimination as running "rings around Gelfand and his attorney"? How did his cowardly silence make "fools of his questioners"? In fact, in the context of the lawsuit, Zborowski's refusal to answer questions on the grounds that his testimony might lead to his own future prosecution supported Gelfand's charge of high-level state penetration of the Socialist Workers Party.

Gelfand's attorneys went back to court to compel Zborowski to answer questions. The hearing on their appeal of Zborowski's invocation of the Fifth Amendment privilege took place on January 4, 1983 before US District Court Magistrate J. Steele Langford. The magistrate responded to John Burton's argument by calling attention to newly passed legislation making it a federal crime to provide information that might lead to the exposure of government agents.

> [The] Court: Now, if you would, why should not the court, in effect, be honoring Mr. Zborowski's concern for indication of the privilege against self-incrimination?
>
> [Mr.] Burton: Your Honor, we—
>
> Court: —In light of the fact that the witness, as I understand it, in part, the deposition, wishes to have this witness identify various persons who were or are in the Socialist Workers Party, which are, in effect, covert agents, perhaps intelligence agents, of the United States?
>
> Burton: Well, that is our cause of action, your Honor, that is to prove that, and we are proceeding to trial March 1 for that exact purpose.
>
> Are you saying would it be a violation of the Intelligence Identities Protection Act?
>
> Court: Yes.[28]

---

27. *The Gelfand Case*, Volume 2, pp. 434–435.
28. Ibid., pp. 465–466.

Magistrate Langford ruled in favor of Zborowski, stating that testimony that led to the exposure of agents in the SWP could lead to his prosecution.

> Now, my feeling is that Mr. Zborowski, given the very nature of this case, when postured up against, since the case was filed, an enactment known as the Protection of Certain National Security Information, which has just become law this year, does or would run a possible risk of violating section 601(a) of that act, were he asked to identify either by name or description or anything else which might lead to the identity of possible intelligence agents who might be superficially participating in this Socialist Workers Party.[29]

Zborowski did not run circles around Gelfand and his attorney, let alone make fools of them. Rather, after a protracted legal struggle, Zborowski was saved, with the critical assistance of his defenders in the Socialist Workers Party, from having to answer their questions by newly passed federal laws that made it a criminal offense to identify government agents inside that organization. Thus ended the only and last opportunity for the Trotskyist movement to interrogate Mark Zborowski.

In a plaintive letter to Albert Glotzer, written on March 1, 1997, you recall: "I tried to see Zborowski several times and phoned him at least four times before he died, but he always hung up on me or shut the door on my face. Swine!" Your indignation was misplaced. Why were you surprised, Ms. Weissman? Did you really expect that Zborowski, a Stalinist agent with blood on his hands, would agree to have a pleasant and informative chat with you about his murders? Did you expect him to bare his soul and seek your understanding? In your naïve approaches to Zborowski, it is you who made a fool of yourself.

Thirty-two years have passed since the conclusion of the Gelfand case. During the past few years, you have advertised yourself as a scholar tirelessly seeking to uncover the truth about the role of Mark Zborowski. You have written, with a tone of weariness, of having "to negotiate a formidable labyrinth of archival censorship and documentation." With a lofty air you proclaim: "Prying secrets loose is never easy." Tell Alan Gelfand and the International

---

29. Ibid., p. 469.

Committee of the Fourth International about that, Ms. Weissman! Rather than being ashamed of your own acquiescence in the lies and cover-ups of Hansen, Novack and Barnes, you are still working to perpetuate them.

In conclusion, I again demand that you publicly retract the slanderous distortions and false statements that appear in the postscript of your article on Mark Zborowski.

Yours sincerely,
David North
National Chairman, Socialist Equality Party (US)
International Editorial Board Chairman of the World Socialist Web Site

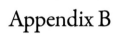

Appendix B

Facsimile Documents

AMERICAN CONSULAR SERVICE

México, D. F., México, September 25, 1940

DEPARTMENT OF STATE

AIR MAIL - Strictly
Confidential

Dear Murphy:

I am resorting again to a personal letter in order
to acquaint you with a desire of Mr. Joseph Hansen,
secretary to the late Mr. Trotsky, to establish confidential
means by which he may be able to communicate with you and
through you to this office from New York City.

Mr. Hansen sails this evening from Veracruz with the
remainder of the late Mr. Trotsky's archives, which are
destined to Harvard University. He will not return to
Mexico. In New York City he may be reached at 116
University Place.

Prior to leaving Mr. Hansen said that he was going
to follow very closely all leads in New York pertaining
to the identity of the assassin of Mr. Trotsky. He
believes it possible that certain information may become
available to him in which the Department will be interested,
and there may develop certain clues which would lead back
to Mexico City, and which could be of value to this office.
For this reason he wishes to be put in touch with someone
in your confidence located in New York to whom confidential
information could be imparted with impunity.

I would greatly appreciate if if you would let me
know the name of the person whom you indicate to Mr. Hansen.

With kind regards,

Sincerely yours,

Geo. P. Shaw

Raymond E. Murphy, Esquire,

Department of State,

Letter dated September 25, 1940, from American Consul to Mexico, George
P. Shaw, to top State Department official Raymond E. Murphy informing
him that Joseph Hansen "wants to be put in touch with someone" in order to
pass on "confidential information" "with impunity."

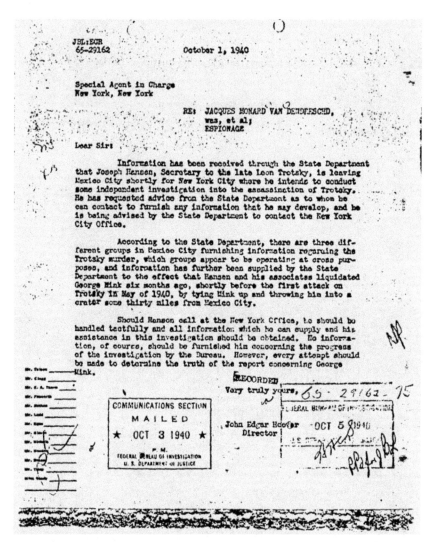

JBL:ECR
65-29162   October 1, 1940

Special Agent in Charge
New York, New York

                    RE: JACQUES MONARD VAN DENDRESCHD,
                         was, et al;
                         ESPIONAGE

Dear Sir:

          Information has been received through the State Department
that Joseph Hansen, Secretary to the late Leon Trotsky, is leaving
Mexico City shortly for New York City where he intends to conduct
some independent investigation into the assassination of Trotsky.
He has requested advice from the State Department as to whom he
can contact to furnish any information that he may develop, and he
is being advised by the State Department to contact the New York
City Office.

          According to the State Department, there are three dif-
ferent groups in Mexico City furnishing information regarding the
Trotsky murder, which groups appear to be operating at cross pur-
poses, and information has further been supplied by the State
Department to the effect that Hansen and his associates liquidated
George Mink six months ago, shortly before the first attack on
Trotsky in May of 1940, by tying Mink up and throwing him into a
crater some thirty miles from Mexico City.

          Should Hansen call at the New York Office, he should be
handled tactfully and all information which he can supply and his
assistance in this investigation should be obtained. No information, of course, should be furnished him concerning the progress
of the investigation by the Bureau. However, every attempt should
be made to determine the truth of the report concerning George
Mink.

                         RECORDED
                         Very truly yours, 65 - 29162 - 15

COMMUNICATIONS SECTION
      MAILED   FEDERAL BUREAU OF INVESTIGATION
   ★ OCT 3 1940 ★   John Edgar Hoover   OCT 5 1940
         P. M.   Director
FEDERAL BUREAU OF INVESTIGATION
U. S. DEPARTMENT OF JUSTICE

Letter from J. Edgar Hoover, October 1, 1940 to New York office of the FBI

RJB:NTP
65-29162- 7 E   October 12, 1940
INDEXED

Special Agent in Charge
New York, New York

            Re: JACQUES MONARD VAN DENDRESCHD
                 was, et al; ESPIONAGE

Dear Sir:

            Reference is made to Bureau letter dated October 1,
1940 wherein you were advised that information had been
received through the State Department to the effect that
Joseph Hansen, secretary to the late Leon Trotsky intended to
leave Mexico City to conduct an independent investigation into
the assassination of Trotsky. He requested advice from the State
Department as to whom he should contact to furnish such information
as he might develop and he was to be advised by the State Department
that he should contact the New York Office.

            For your further information in connection with this
matter, I am enclosing herewith copies of a letter which was
directed to Mr. Little of the Bureau on September 28, 1940 by
Mr. R. E. Murphy. It will be noted from this letter that Joseph
Hansen was sailing from Vera Cruz on September 25, 1940 and he had
in his possession Trotsky's archives which are to be delivered to
Harvard University. It will also be noted that Hansen's address
while in New York City will be 116 University Place.

            You are requested to have an Agent interview Mr. Hansen
for information which would be of assistance in connection with
the investigation of this case. An effort should be made to verify
or disprove the report of the death of George Mink. You should,
of course, refrain from furnishing any information to Hansen concerning
the Bureau's investigation and this interview should be conducted
in a most discreet manner.

                                        Very truly yours,

COMMUNICATIONS SECTION
MAILED
* OCT 12 1940 *
P. M
FEDERAL BUREAU OF INVESTIGATION
U. S. DEPARTMENT OF JUSTICE

                                        John Edgar Hoover
                                        Director
Enclosures

Letter from J. Edgar Hoover, October 12, 1940 to New York office of the FBI

October 23, 1940

Mr. Geo. P. Shaw
American Consul
American Consulate General
Mexico, D.F., Mexico

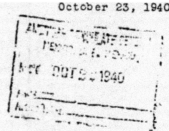

Dear Mr. Shaw,

       I received your letter concerning Mr. Sackett in good condition and shall visit him shortly.

       There was a little delay in my receiving your communication due to my absence from New York for some days while I was at Boston.

       Respectfully,

       Joseph Hansen

Joseph Hansen
116 University Pl.
New York City, N.Y.

Letter from Joseph Hansen to George P. Shaw, US Consul in Mexico City, dated October 23, 1940, thanking him "respectfully" for arranging his confidential contact with the FBI.

62-6870

had no connection with the May 24th affair, and
the fact that he had given Sylvia the address of
the Ermita Building — of all places in Mexico City,
a city he was visiting for the first time in his
life — was · pure chance.'

'I gave her the first address that came to my
mind," said Jacsoncboly.'"

The aforementioned issue of "Labor Action" is being
retained in the files of the New York Office.

In letter dated October 1, 1940, the Bureau advised
that JOSEPH HANSEN, Secretary to the late Leon Trotsky, was
leaving Mexico City shortly for New York City, where he intended conducting independent investigation into the assassination of Trotsky. He requested advice from the State Department
as to whom he could contact to furnish any information he may
develop and was being advised by the State Department to contact
this office. It is further stated that information was
supplied by the State Department that HANSEN and his associates
liquidated GEORGE MINK six months ago, shortly before the first
attack on Trotsky in May, 1940, by tying MINK up and throwing
him into a crater some thirty miles from Mexico City.

The writer made several attempts to contact JOSEPH
HANSEN at the headquarters of the Socialist Workers Party,
Section of the Fourth International, 116 University Place,
(fourth floor), New York City, but without success. It was
not until Special Agent C. J. STARR made a personal telephone
call to JAMES P. CANNON, Party Secretary, that an interview was
arranged.

The writer interviewed JAMES P. CANNON and JOSEPH HANSEN
regarding the Trotsky affair and was advised by them that they
had no information to offer. They appeared very reluctant to
discuss the matter and gave very brief answers to questions put
to them by reporting agent. A further interview will be had
with these men, at which time an effort will be made to secure
information that they may have regarding this affair.

With regard to the alleged death of GEORGE MINK in
Mexico, the writer was informed by confidential informant

-8-

December 9, 1940 report by FBI Special Agent M.R. Griffin, regarding the request by Joseph Hansen for a contact to whom he could "furnish any information he may develop..." Agent Griffin refers to information "supplied by the State Department that HANSEN and his associates liquidated GEORGE MINK six months ago..." The agent relates that, when interviewed at the SWP offices, Cannon and Hansen advised him "that they had no information to offer."

ROY T. NOONAN, recalled as a witness by the Government,
testified as follows:

Direct Examination by Mr. Schweinhaut

I am Inspection Agent R.T. Noonan of the F.B.I., who
has previously testified in this case. When we executed the
search warrant on June 27, 1941, at the St. Paul headquarters of
the Socialist Workers Party, we found and took with us some copies
of the Declaration of Principles and Constitution of the Party.
The F.B.I. office in St. Paul has had several investigations of
the Socialist Workers Party in their files for the past years.
In the latter part of 1940 there were two or three specific investigations, and in this case it was intensified in February of this

-371-

Trial transcript of Agent Roy T. Noonan's testimony in the 1941 trial of the SWP "18," p. 371

year. Tommy Williams was interviewed by agents of the F.B.I. in
this case in February, 1941. He is now dead. I understand he
died March 10, 1941.

Cross Examination by Mr. Goldman

There were other books in the St. Paul office which we
did not take and of which I did not make a list. I don't remember
all of the other books. I don't know whether there were any books
dealing with poetry or literature. This investigation started
before I came into the St. Paul office. It started in February
or March, 1941. We have had information regarding some of the
defendants before then. I know we had it in November, 1940.

Q. Do you know that your superior received instructions
from Washington after a telegram was sent to Washington by President Tobin of the International to continue the investigation and
to get an indictment?

MR. ANDERSON: I object to that as incompetent, irrelevant and immaterial and not proper cross examination.

THE COURT: Sustained. I don't see what difference it
makes what this man knew about it. He was directed to go ahead and
make the investigation.

MR. GOLDMAN: But the question of investigation and the
motives for it --

THE COURT: That is right. He doesn't determine the
motives that actuated the investigation.

The witness, continuing:

I talked to about fifty people in the course of my investigation and I would say about 25 of them were members of 544
• • • • • • •

Trial transcript of Agent Roy T. Noonan's testimony in the 1941 trial of the
SWP "18", p. 372

Federal Bureau of Investigation
United States Department of Justice
Washington, D. C.

5

RECEIVED
MAY 6 1943
CRIMINAL DIVISION

MEMORANDUM FOR ASSISTANT ATTORNEY GENERAL
WENDELL BERGE

RE: SOCIALIST WORKERS PARTY

   Information has been received that on the evening of April 30,
1943, members of the subject organization picketed the opening of the
film "Mission to Moscow" playing at the Hollywood Theater, Times Square,
New York City.

   In connection with this picket, six females carried placards
containing such titles as "Stalin is the Real Defendant in the Moscow
Trials," "Mission to Moscow - Stalin's Crimes Against Labor," and "The
John Dewey Commission Hearing Branded Moscow Trials as Frame Ups."
Other individuals distributed pamphlets reportedly setting forth a
summary of the findings of the John Dewey Commission. This pamphlet
also allegedly stated that the reason for the film was to do a diplomatic
favor for Stalin and to whitewash his crimes in return for Stalin's
support of the Allied powers. James P. Cannon, National Secretary of
the Socialist Workers Party, and approximately twenty other members of
the Party were present at the picketing but did not participate. Many
of the pamphlets mentioned above were distributed to members of the
Armed Forces.

   Copies of the above-mentioned pamphlet are being obtained and
will be made available to you at a future date.

   The above is being submitted for your information and to keep
you currently advised concerning the activities of the subject group.

     Very truly yours,

       John Edgar Hoover

J. Edgar Hoover to Assistant Attorney General Wendell Berge, May 1943

United States Department of Justice
Federal Bureau of Investigation
Washington 25, D. C.

PERSONAL AND CONFIDENTIAL

June 12, 1948

MEMORANDUM FOR THE ATTORNEY GENERAL

RE: SOCIALIST WORKERS PARTY.
INTERNAL SECURITY - SWP

The Socialist Workers Party will hold its National
Convention at the Irving Plaza Hotel from July 1 through 5, 1948,
and it is believed possible to cover the various sessions of the
Convention by technical means.

As you know, the Socialist Workers Party is a militant
Trotskyite group and as dangerous if not more so to the internal
security than the Communist Party. At the present time an extensive investigation is being conducted of the Socialist Workers
Party and the coverage of this National Convention is believed
desirable.

It is requested, therefore, that you authorize the use
of technical equipment in connection with our surveillance work
of the National Convention of the Socialist Workers Party at the
Irving Plaza Hotel, New York City, from July 1 through 5, 1948.

Respectfully,

John Edgar Hoover
Director

FILED
BY
ON JAN 30 956

Orig. appvd. as above and ret. to FBI. 6-15-48

146-1-10

DEPARTMENT OF JUSTICE
JAN 12 1956

CONFIDENTIAL

June 12, 1948 Letter from J. Edgar Hoover requesting the 1948 SWP
National Convention be bugged

The Attorney General   July 7, 1948

Director, FBI

SOCIALIST WORKERS PARTY
INTERNAL SECURITY - SWP
FBI File No. 100-16-35

    A reliable confidential source has advised that the Socialist Workers Party convention started about 11:00 a.m. on July 1, 1948, at the Irving Plaza Hall, 15 Irving Place, New York City. About 300 people are attending the convention from various branches in the United States, as well as representatives from Canada, England and Latin America. The first speaker at the convention was Morris Lewitt, National Organisational Secretary of the Socialist Workers Party, who gave a report on the international situation and the World Congress of the Fourth International. He stated that the World Congress started on April 2, 1948, and lasted for three weeks. He stated that he attended the Congress as the Socialist Workers Party representative and Grace Chin Lee attended as the representative of the Johnson faction of the Socialist Workers Party.

    It was reported that a resolution was adopted declaring an end to unity negotiations between the Socialist Workers Party and the Workers Party and stating that the Workers Party is not a section of the Fourth International. It was reported that the Johnson faction issue was settled with this faction of the Socialist Workers Party, consisting of about 84 members, agreeing with the Socialist Workers Party majority to defend the Union of Soviet Socialist Republics in the event of war between the United States and the USSR. This source indicated that there are approximately 1,500 members in the Socialist Workers Party in the United States at this time. The instant confidential source advised that on July 2, 1948, there were 97 delegates and 63 alternates from 23 states represented at the Socialist Workers Party convention.

    The second day was devoted to a discussion led by William F. Ward on the militarisation of the United States and the tasks of the Fourth International. Ward stated that the Party should advocate that the people in the United States vote on the question of universal military training and it was indicated that he felt that youths who are old enough to fight are also old enough to vote. George Clarke, Socialist Workers Party National Campaign Manager, made an appeal for $25,000 to help in the Presidential campaign. Pledges from the various branches amounted to $23,000.

    An additional reliable confidential source advised that Grace Chin Lee gave the minority report on the World Congress of the Fourth International, stating that Max Shachtman of the Workers Party was expelled and that after much confusion, the Congress ended successfully.

Internal FBI informants' report on SWP 1948 National Convention

NY 100-4019

German Section

According to information supplied by Confidential Informant T-1, the IEC passed a resolution concerning the IKD (German Section). The IEC after hearing the report of Comrade J. and discussing the letter addressed to Comrade J. by the leading members of the IKD, decided that these Comrades despite repeated invitations from the IEC and IS to collaborate with them in reorganizing the German Section, have refused to recognize the IEC and IS and to conduct themselves as other disciplined sections of the International.

The resolution further states that the Comrades of the IKD have declared that they will accept only conditionally the political and organizational discipline of the next Congress of the International. The IEC decided that in spite of the above action on the part of the IKD that it would make an exception and grant the IKD permission to participate as one of the German Sections in the International discussion and at the World Congress.

British Party

The IEC also adopted a resolution on the British question reaffirming the line adopted at the June Plenum in 1946 and approving the letter addressed by the IS to the Central Committee of the Revolutionary Communist Party.

T-1 advised that Comrade HASTON issued a substitute resolution on the British question but that this resolution was rejected. HASTON's resolution requested the IEC to decide against having the RCP membership infiltrate into the British Labor Party and instead request the principal orientation of the membership towards the trade unions with the object of having the RCP membership penetrate these basic organizations of the working class.

Greek Party

According to T-1, the IEC adopted a resolution recognizing the ICP as the official Greek Section of the 4th International retroactive to the date of the Greek Unification Congress of July 1946. This resolution pointed out further that at the IEC 2nd Plenum of October 1946 a resolution

- 7 -

Example of informant reports on international sections of the Fourth International

Palestine

The Palestine Section is reported to be headed by one CLIFF. However, the informant reported that most of the Trotskyist elements in Palestine are attempting to get out of Palestine and into other European countries where they can better spread their propaganda.

Egypt

Informant reported that although many leaders of the movement in Egypt had been arrested, there is a very strong section of the Fourth International in this part of the world.

Africa

Informant reported that the movement's activities had been hampered greatly by police work in this country.

Ceylon

Informant said that the movement is doing very good work among the natives here and one source reported there were approximately 2,000 members.

China

The informant stated that a comrade by the name of RILEY had done a great deal of work in the Far East.

Bulgaria

The informant had no information concerning the section in this country.

Greece

Informant stated that although it is known that the Fourth International has a section in this country, the strength and activities are unknown at this time.

Germany

The informant stated that the movement had a section in Lubeck and one in Hamburg, as well as at least three other groups in this country.

Further reports on international activities of the Trotskyist movement

ARNE SWABECK, alias Arn Swabek
2551 N. Laramie, Chicago

SWABECK was at one time a full-time functionary of the SWP
in New York City and, according to CGO 5644, was elected a member of the
SWP National Committee on November 18, 1946 at the National Convention
in Chicago. According to CGO 5625, SWABECK continues to participate in
activities of the SWP in Chicago and apparently is one of the leading
policy makers.

MEYER JAMES MYER, alias Meyer Lebovsky,
Mike Meyer, Mike Michaels
3609 Dickens Street

MYER was born July 15, 1905 in Russia and was naturalized
January 27, 1928 in Chicago. He is an attorney with offices at 77 W.
Washington Street and, according to CGO 5625, has regularly acted in a
legal capacity for the SWP and for Front organizations of the SWP including recently the Hickman Defense Committee and the Chicago Tenants
Federation. He acted as one of the Defense attorneys during the trial
of eighteen SWP members during 1942 at Minneapolis, Minnesota, in which
they were convicted of conspiracy to advocate the overthrow of the U. S.
Government. MYER has been a member of the Local Executive Committee in
Chicago and, according to CGO 5625, regularly participates in the activities of the SWP in Chicago. CGO 5625 also has advised that MYER is now
married to BELLE MYER who formerly was known as BELLE ROSEN and who was
the wife of JACK A. ROSEN, Chicago SWP member.

BELLE MYER
3609 Dickens

As indicated above, BELLE MYER was formerly BELLE ROSEN.
During and prior to the SWP convention held in Chicago in November,
1946, she was very active in making arrangements for this convention
and she reportedly is Secretary-Treasurer of the Chicago Local of the
SWP. She also has served as Chairman of the Emergency Relief Committee
of the SWP.

DAVID BEN COOPER, alias David Robb
1523 W. Melrose

COOPER is employed by the Wieboldt Stores, Inc., in Chicago
where, according to CGO 5625, he recently has been active in organizing

Example of detailed FBI report on individual SWP members from the
Chicago branch

INDEX

ALEXANDER, ANNE	18,21,23,25,26,27, 28,36,37,38,42,43,44, 45,47,48
ALLEN, ELLA	6
ANGLEMEIR, ANNE	9
ANGLEMEIR, KENNETH MORTON	6,21,22
AZIZ, INOUS A.	67
BAILY, M.A.	7
BALLARD, ANNE	6,7,8
BARBARIA, FRANK ANTHONY	4,7,18,21,38,43,49,52,53,55, 56,57,60,61
BARGES, LOIS	66
BARNETT, HOWARD	6,8
BARTON, FRED	6,54,56,57,59,60
BECKER, ARTHUR	6,7,9
BELL, ADA	29
BELL, AL	6,45,66
BELL, MARY ANNE	8,28
BERNARD, GUY	6
BERNARD, LILY	6
BERG, BEATRICE	5
BERG, DAVE	5,40,50,62
BERG, HENRY	7,8,9,52,53
BLACK, H.	7,19
BRAUN,	5
BRONSON, ART	6
BROWN, CALVIN	65
CHASE, BOB	7
CHERTOV, ANNE	6,18,21,23,25,26,27,28,36, 37,38,42,43,44,45,47,48
CHERTOV, ROBERT	3,4,6,8,15,16,18,21,22,23, 25,26,27,28,36,37,38,41, 42,43,44,45,47,48,49,52, 53,54,55,56,57,60,63,64,68
CHESTER, ANNE	6,8
CHESTER, BOB	3,4,6,7,9,17,18,21,23,25, 26,27,36,37,38,39,41,42, 43,44,45,47,48,54,55,56,57, 59,60,63,64
COCHRAN, BOB	5,7,9
COCHRAN, LINDELL	5,9

-1-C

FBI report on an SWP branch with index for references to individual members

C - S P Political Committee Meeting of August 5, 1947

Confidential Informant T-14, a highly confidential source, not in a position to testify, furnished temporarily a copy of a document entitled: "DISCUSSIONS ON WORLD CONGRESS – PC MEETING, August 5, 1947". This document which is believed to be a discussion at a political committee meeting of the SWP reflected that MORRIS LEWITT, under his alias of STEIN, led the discussion at this meeting, pointing out that the World Congress is the most important gathering of the Fourth International to date and that in STEIN's opinion it even exceeds the founding conference in importance.

Report from "Confidential Informant T-14, a highly confidential source, not in a position to testify" regarding SWP Political Committee meetings

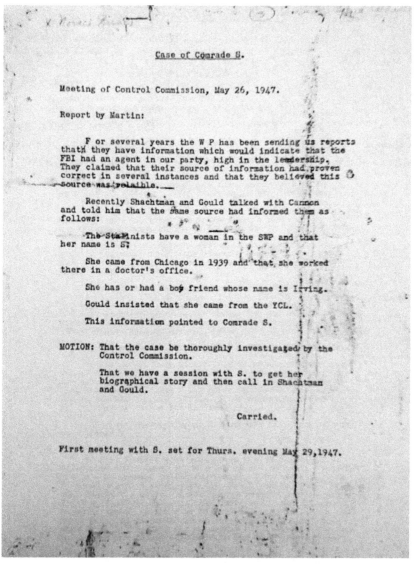

Case of Comrade S.

Meeting of Control Commission, May 26, 1947.

Report by Martin:

    F or several years the W P has been sending us reports that they have information which would indicate that the FBI had an agent in our party, high in the leadership. They claimed that their source of information had proven correct in several instances and that they believed this source was reliable.

    Recently Shachtman and Gould talked with Cannon and told him that the same source had informed them as follows:

    The Stalinists have a woman in the SWP and that her name is S.

    She came from Chicago in 1939 and that she worked there in a doctor's office.

    She has or had a boy friend whose name is Irving.

    Gould insisted that she came from the YCL.

    This information pointed to Comrade S.

MOTION: That the case be thoroughly investigated by the
        Control Commission.

        That we have a session with S. to get her
        biographical story and then call in Shachtman
        and Gould.

                          Carried.

First meeting with S. set for Thurs. evening May 29,1947.

Minutes of the SWP Control Commission, May 26, 1947, p.1

MEETING with Comrade S

Case of Comrade S.

May 29, 1947.

In response to questions put to her by members of
the Secretariat and Control Cimmission in combined session,
the following biographical sketch was given:

My father's name is John Callen. He has been a
salesman for many years. Neither he nor any other member
of my family entertain or ever entertained any political
views other than the average citizen.

I myself did not know that there was such a thing
as a radical movement until I was about 19, at college.

I lived in Milwaukee until about 1932. I went to
Madison,Wisc. to attend the University of Wisconsin. There
I met Zalmond Franklin and we got married in February 1935.
We were together on and off for about ayear. I graduated
J une 1935 and left school. Franklin remained at school.
After graduatingI looked for work and finally found a job
in a Milwaukee drug store and worked there for a while as
sales clerk.

In the Fall of 1935 or Spring of 1936 I went to
Chicago to live with my folks. There I entered the Chicago
University to study social service. I went to school there
for four quarters, working one summer for the Jewish Social
Service outfit there, and then went to work for the Chicago
Relief Administration where I worked until I came to New York.

In the summer of 1937 I joined a YPSL circle in Chicago.

I came to New York in May 1938 to go to work for the
Hebrew Association for the Deaf. I worked part time there
and helped out in the National Office of the SWP in spare
time. In December 1938 I was asked to take a full-time
job in the SWP National Office as the office secretary
was leaving to take a job in industry.

On direct questioning of Cannon, the following answers
were given:

My fist contact with radicalism was at Wisconsin
University where there was a group of the National Students'
League. My husband joined the League, 1935 semester, and
I joined too just because he did. But I really didn't know
what it was all about. I don't know whether the YCL had a
fraction there at the time, but there was a radical group,
bohemian types, of which my husband was none, and which was
considered the "Communists" on the campus. I never knew
whether my husband had any communist affiliations, but knew
he was radical in his views and he may have been a member.

Minutes of the SWP Control Commission, May 26, 1947, p.2

2   Case of S.

I do know that his parents were either communists in ideology
or just on the fringe of the Communist Party. They once gave
a house party for the F riends of the Soviet Union.

Some years ago I heard that my former husband had been
in Spain during the revolutionary days there. So I imagine
he must have become a YCLer after our separation. Or he may
very likely have been one before. I did not know enough
then to be able to detect that and he never trusted me with
any information about his activities.
                                  ever
" Did you/belong to the YCL ?"

No, never. I knew of the existence of such an organization but reacted against it emotionally because of the
Bohemian character of the people around my husband who were
considered "communists". But I did not really understand
what communism was.

" How did you come to join the YPSL? Any member of your
family interested in Socialism?"

No, none of my family ever had or have now any
radical views. I came to join the YPSL chiefly I guess,
because I was so lonely. I did not fit in with the friends
of my family and I had no circle of my own. At the University
in Madison, I got my first contact with radicalism and in
a vague way I got to feel that socialism is a good thing.
I heard Norman Thomas speak a t the Socialist Club of the
University of Chicago and he made a deep impression on me.
I wanted to know more about socialism, so in my loneliness,
I consulted the Chicago telephone directory for the address
of some socialisr organization, and founf the Socialist
Bookstore.

At the time, I was working as a social worker in Chicago..
The work I was doing, by the way, did not help me any. The
patronizing attitude toward the poor was very distasteful
to me.   W ell, so I went to the Socialist Party bookstore
for some of their literature. There I met Lydia Beidel.
She told me about the Young People's Socialist League in
my neighborhood and invited me to attend. I went. They met
a t Belle's house. There I met a number of people. They
seemed so different from the people I had known and made
me feel so at home that I returned to a number of meetin gs
and then joined the Circle. They were different from the
other type of radicals I had known at college and I liked
them as people. In the summer of 1937 I joined the YPSL
circle on the North Side, Chicago.

P aul Picquet was the organizer of this circle. Most
of the members of this circle were already Trotskyists. I
came under their influence.

Several months after the F ounding Convention of the

Minutes of the SWP Control Commission, May 26, 1947, p.3

3   Case of S.

Socialist Workers Party.   I joined the party. The branch
I joined had in it Goldman, Belle, H elen Judd, Shirley S,
Irving Bern and all the other Landaus.

When I left for New York I was transferred. Here I was
attached to the Village Branch which met at Luttinger's.
In this branch was Rose Karsner, Frieda Moore, Billie Ramloff.

" Did you ever work for a doctor in Chicago or Milwaukee?"

No, never. The only doctor I knew in those days was
my husband's father. But I never worked for any doctor.

" Did you ever have a boy friend by the name of Irving?"

I may have casually known some student by that name,
though I don't recall any. But I never had any close
friend by that name.

Minutes of the SWP Control Commission, May 26, 1947, p.4

Case of Comrade S.

June 5, 1947.

Joint meeting of Control Comm. and Secretariat.

PURPOSE of meeting: To hear a report from WP members about
rumors concerning comrade S which came
to their attention.

Report by Shachtman: " About one, two or three weeks
after Budenz's book, THIS IS MY STORY came out, a reliable
friend of ours came and told me that an FBI agent called on
him to get some information. In the course of the conversation
the FBI man told our friend Jones that the Stalinists have
an agent in the SWP. He then asked if Jones knew a certain
"S" in the SWP who came from Chicago in 1939, got a job in
the office of the SWP and then became private secretary
to Cannon. In Chicago she worked for a doctor. She had a
Stalinist boy friend by the name of Irving. "

The WP comrades were then told of "S"'s biographical
sketch as it was given to us by her.

Comrade G of the WP then told of the first time he
met "S" at a membership meeting in Chicago in the NW side,
about 1937.

The WP members assured us they had not talked to anyone
about the matter and would not do so. They agreed there
was nothing in the information they had except the statement
of an FBI man, but felt duty-bound to report the matter to us.

Cannon pointed out that the only facts upon which the
FBI man based the conclusion that she is a Stalinist agent
in the SWP were:

1- That comrade S came to New York from Chicago in 1939.
2- That she had worked for a doctor in Chicago
3- That she got a job as stenographer in the office of
the SWP and later became Cannon's private secretary.
4- That she had or has a boy friend named Irving.

Discussion followed and the general consensus of opinion
was that the above points did not constitute any facts upon
which to base any credence in the rumor or further action.

After the WP members left the discussion was continued
and the following motion was made and carried:

MOTION: That there is no basis for suspicion of comrade S
in the statements of the FBI man and that we so notify comrade S,

Minutes of the SWP Control Commission, May 26, 1947, p.5

2 Case of comrade S   June 5

        That we make no mention of the case to anyone and
ask the WP comrades not to speak of it either.

        That we watch for evidence of any gossip about this
matter and in the event that such gossip develops we act
promptly according to the circumstances dictated by the
new developments.

                                    Rose Karsner, Secy.
                                    Control Commission

Minutes of the SWP Control Commission, May 26, 1947, p.6

Chicago, Ill.
August 21, 1950

Dear Jim,

I have seen S. When I showed her the passage in the Budenz book and told her of the Shachtmanite prattle she reacted with mingled anger against her detractors and anxiety for her family.

She told me the FBI has been hounding her and her family. As a result her father almost lost his job and was told that if there is any more investigating he will be fired. The FBI tried to question her about the party but she refused to give them any information.

Her family now knows the whole score and they have put heavy pressure on her to keep her away from the movement.

She does not want to be involved either directly or indirectly in the matter of a reply to Budenz. I asked if she would be willing to sit down with Mike and me to help us gather some of the facts needed to refute Budenz which would be used without openly or directly involving her. She said she did not want to be drawn into the thing in any manner whatever.

I told her we considered it absolutely necessary to reply to Budenz charges. She asked if we couldn't just issue a statement announcing that a full investigation of his allegations was made three years ago which proved his story false and denounce him as a character assassin. She asked if the statement couldn't be general, i.e., not refer to any specific person in refuting him, but state that no such person as he describes has ever been in the party office.

She appeared to be in good health, seemed pleased to see me, and she asked about everyone. She had not heard about Oscar.

So far as I can see there is no point in attempting to press her any further on this matter. It seems best to go ahead along the lines we agreed on when we discussed the question in the secretariat right after the last plenum.

Farrell

Farrell

Farrell Dobbs' 1950 letter to James Cannon concerning his discussion with Sylvia Callen

Cannon's letter to his wife, Rose Karsner, 1960, page 1

I have left the house only a few times in the month since I returned. Dinner twice at Walta's, dinner out twice with Steve and Pamela — That's all. I take Blackie for his walk every day. He sticks close to me in the house all the time, and makes it clear that he feels something is missing. Every once in a while he sniffs at the closed door of your room and then flops down beside it in the hall as though waiting for you to come out.

Julia shops for me and I have no trouble about food. Except for salads, I am more or less back on my routine diet. The other night I cooked a T-bone steak. Blackie enjoyed the bone so much, went at it so enthusiastically, that it made my own meal taste better.

Reba dropped me a note today about your anti-biotic treatments to clear up your cold. I would like to get reports from you on the progress of your other treatments.

Love ever, Jim

Cannon's letter to his wife, Rose Karsner, 1960, page 2

POLITICAL COMMITTEE MEETING No. 8   April 16, 1983

Present: Barnes, Budka, Clark, Gannon, González, Jaquith, Leonard,
           Lovell, Morell, Pérez, Seigle, Shilman, Studer, Warren,
           Waters

Absent: Jenness (leadership school), Miah (Chicago)

Guests: Goodman, Jayko, Lyons, Sandler, Sheppard

Convened: 9:00 a.m.

Chair: Lovell

Agenda: 1. Gelfand-Pfaelzer-Fisher/Moest Case
           2. Héctor Marroquín Defense Campaign
           3. Tax Exempt Status for PRDF Incorporated
           4. Mandel Rejoinder to Jenness
           5. International Internal Discussion Bulletin
           6. National Committee Meeting and Scheduling of Party
              Conventions and Activists and Educational Conference
           7. Turkish Emergency Defense Campaign

1. GELFAND-PFAELZER-FISHER/MOEST CASE

   Seigle reported on perspectives for ongoing legal work and political
campaign around Gelfand-Pfaelzer-Fisher/Moest case. For months leading
up to trial and through the trial and preparation of post trial legal
offensive, Political Committee decided to subordinate all other
matters involving allocation of leadership resources and attention
to preparation of trial and defense work. Now we can readjust our
assignments.

   Continuing legal work will demand leadership attention, however.
We will shortly submit our proposed "findings of fact" to Judge
Pfaelzer, constituting our proposals for content of her written
decision in the case. This will fundamentally contain two aspects:
1) that Gelfand failed to substantiate his charges of a government
takeover of SWP and its leadership; and 2) that the case was
orchestrated and financed by the Workers Revolutionary Party in
collaboration with Gelfand for purpose of disruption and harassment
of the SWP.

   In addition to proposed "findings of fact," we will file
motion for costs and attorneys' fees to be assessed against both
Gelfand and the Fisher & Moest law firm.

   No further court appearances are currently scheduled. It would
normally take several months for these rulings to be handed down,
after which Gelfand and Fisher & Moest may appeal.

   Seigle also reported on proposals to continue campaign around
case in several ways:

   1) The need to follow up on collection of pledges to PRDF fund.
Some $100,000 has been pledged, but only half has been collected.
Most outstanding pledges are from party members. Collection of the
remaining funds quickly is critical for PRDF.

SWP Political Committee Meeting Minutes, April 16, 1983, page 1
(Wisconsin Historical Society)

2) Some support work remains to be done, especially in Los Angeles and on a national level. We want to follow up on endorsement requests that were initiated before Pfaelzer's favorable ruling. We do not project a continuing national campaign to get new endorsers at this stage. When Gelfand and/or Fisher & Moest appeal, however, we will review that perspective.

3) We need to explain the success of the party's political campaign to win support around this case and what that registers about political changes in the U.S. class struggle. This campaign was a victory for the SWP. We found many fighters in the labor movement, Black struggle, etc. who readily understood the stakes in the case and how the government uses the courts against the working class and oppressed nationalities. The case divided liberals, with some refusing to support the case, since they believe the courts have a legitimate role in such matters.

We want to do one or more Militant articles rounding up the lessons of the campaign and its political significance, along with news articles on continuing legal developments.

We are also preparing an article for Intercontinental Press on the political degeneration of the Healyites, anchored in their sectarian reaction against the Cuban revolution and its proletarian leadership.

Finally, we should write an article presenting the party's position on the accusations against Sylvia Caldwell. The article should present for the party and the international movement our political position on the responsibility of the party to defend itself against Cointelpro-type "snitch-jacket" operations of the kind that is now being carried out against Sylvia Caldwell and the SWP. It is especially necessary to explain again, for those who have never learned or have forgotten, the responsibility of the leadership of a revolutionary workers party to defend loyally each and every member against such slander campaigns.

The article will examine the new "evidence" produced by the FBI in Pfaelzer's courtroom and circulated by the WL/WRP, consisting of what is presented as transcripts of testimony given by Sylvia Caldwell before two grand juries investigating Soviet "espionage" in the 1950s. We have no way of knowing how much the transcripts are doctored. Moreover, testimony given under those conditions -- before a secret grand jury, without a lawyer, under threat of indictment as a Soviet spy in the shadow of the judicial murder of Ethel and Julius Rosenberg -- cannot be taken as true by any serious workers' leader.

Because of inexperience and some confusion on these points, in the party and in the international movement, an article along these lines would be helpful.

Discussion

SWP Political Committee Meeting Minutes, April 16, 1983, page 2 (Wisconsin Historical Society)

11 June 1982

MEMORANDUM FOR: Executive Director

FROM: Stanley Sporkin
General Counsel

SUBJECT: Weekly OGC Report for the DCI/DDCI

ITEMS OF MAJOR INTEREST - 5 - 11 JUNE 1982

Procedures Implementing E.O 12333. Attorney General Smith has signed the new procedures governing CIA activities outside the United States and the procedures relating to the conduct of counterintelligence activities outside the United States by the FBI. Upon the signing by the DCI of the procedures governing CIA activities abroad, both sets will be forwarded by CIA to the Senate and House Intelligence Committees, and both will become effective in seven days.

Judicial Decision Supporting Secrecy of Identities of Intelligence Personnel. In Gelfand v. Attorney General, DCI, et al, Gelfand claims that alleged CIA and FBI agents in the Socialist Workers Party (SWP) expelled him from the Party. In pretrial discovery, Gelfand submitted interrogatories asking the DCI whether 19 named SWP members are or have been CIA agents and whether CIA believes that one named individual is a Soviet intelligence agent. The DCI refused to answer the interrogatories on the ground that answering them would tend to reveal intelligence activities, sources, and methods. The U.S. District Court hearing the case upheld the DCI's refusal to answer, holding that the DCI's statutory responsibility to protect intelligence sources and methods and the CIA's statutory exemption from any requirement to disclose the names or functions of CIA personnel justify the refusal to answer. The Gelfand case is the second case in what appears to be a developing trend in the law of recognizing a DCI/CIA statutory privilege against disclosure of intelligence identities in pretrial civil discovery.

Legislative Developments. On Thursday, 10 June, the Senate approved the conference report on H.R. 4, the Intelligence Identities Protection Act, by a vote of 81 to 4. The Senate action clears the legislation for the President's signature.

The Senate Judiciary Subcommittee on Agency Administration met on Wednesday, 10 June, to mark up S. 1775, which would amend the Federal Tort Claims Act to substitute the U.S. Government for its employees as the defendant in cases based upon employees' acts performed within the scope of their

Recently declassified 1982 CIA memo protecting the agency's "statutory exemption from any requirement to disclose names or functions of CIA personnel..."

Timeline of Major Events of the *Security and the Fourth International* Investigation

Mid 1930s	Trotskyist movement in US on the FBI's list for "Custodial Detention," i.e., round up and detention in case of national emergency
August 1936	First Moscow Trial: "Trial of the Sixteen" (includes Zinoviev and Kamenev)
November 1936	GPU breaks into the Nikolaevsky Institute library in Paris with the help of Mark Zborowski ("Etienne") to steal Trotsky's papers
January 1937	Second Moscow Trial: Trial of the Anti-Soviet Trotskyite Center (Radek-Pyatakov)
January 1937	Trotsky arrives in Mexico and is greeted by official Mexican delegation, headed by President Lazaro Cardenas
End of 1936-beginning of 1937	Dr. Gregory Rabinowitz, GPU spy leader in New York City, instructs Louis Budenz to meet Sylvia Callen in Chicago and integrate her into the Trotskyist movement as a GPU agent
July 1937	Erwin Wolf, Trotsky's political secretary, abducted and then murdered by GPU in Barcelona, Spain

September 4, 1937	Ignatz Reiss, GPU defector who declared support for Trotsky, murdered by GPU outside of Lausanne
February 1938	Lev Sedov, Trotsky's son, murdered by GPU in Paris, France
March 1938	Third Moscow Trial: "Trial of the Twenty-One" (Bukharin-Rakovsky)
July 1938	Rudolf Klement, secretary of the Fourth International, murdered by GPU in Paris, France
September 3, 1938	Founding congress of the Fourth Interntional outside Paris
1938	Joseph Hansen meets with GPU agent in New York City
May 24, 1940	First raid of Trotsky residence in Coyoacan, orchestrated by GPU, led by painter David Alfaro Siqueiros; GPU agent Robert Sheldon Harte lets attackers in; he is later found murdered
August 20, 1940	Trotsky mortally wounded by Mercader
August 21, 1940	Trotsky dies
August 31, 1940	Hansen begins communicating with United States government
September 25, 1940	American Consul George P. Shaw notifies State Department that Hansen "wants to be put in touch with someone" in order to pass on "confidential information" "with impunity"
October 1940	J. Edgar Hoover encourages FBI to develop relationship with Hansen
November 1940	FBI investigation reaches new level—high internal sources acquired, according to Special Agent Roy Noonan
December 9, 1940	FBI Special Agent M.R. Griffin notes he went to SWP headquarters to discuss Trotsky assassination but Cannon and Hansen were "very reluctant to discuss the matter"
February-March 1941	FBI infiltration of SWP "intensified" according to Special Agent Roy Noonan
June 1941	J. Edgar Hoover continues to demand Justice Department prosecute SWP. That month, US

	Attorneys in charge of investigation and Teamster President Daniel Tobin also appeal for prosecution
June 22, 1941	Nazi Germany invades Soviet Union
June 23, 1941	Roosevelt administration makes decision to prosecute SWP
June 27, 1941	FBI raids headquarters of Minneapolis branch of SWP
November 1941	Trial of the twenty-eight SWP defendants in Minneapolis, Minnesota. Grant Dunne killed himself on the eve of the trial
December 1, 1941	Eighteen SWP members convicted for violating the Smith Act; jury recommends leniency
December 7, 1941	Japanese attack Pearl Harbor, Hawaii
December 8, 1941	"The 18" are sentenced to federal prison for between twelve and eighteen months.
December 1943	After losing appeal and after Supreme Court declined review, the SWP 18 begin their jail sentences. (Ultimately released after six or twelve months)
March 1947	SWP receives advanced copy of Louis Budenz's 1947 book *This is My Story*
March 8, 1947	The *Militant* carries banner headline: "Stalin's guilt in Trotsky murder bared by ex-Daily Worker editor"
March 17, 1947	SWP organizes coalition including Norman Thomas, James T. Farrell, John Dewey, and Sidney Hook, who present petition to Manhattan district attorney demanding grand jury convention to investigate Budenz revelations
May 1947	Shachtman and Glotzer visit SWP headquarters in New York
May 26, 1947	SWP Control Commission meets to consider "the Case of Comrade S." for first time
May 29, 1947	Control Commission meets for second time, interviews Sylvia Callen
June 5, 1947	Control Commission swears those present to silence, absolves Callen. Callen abandons SWP and leaves New York City shortly thereafter

June 5, 1947	Budenz finally appears before grand jury but SWP drops the matter entirely
1950	Budenz publishes second book, *Men Without Faces*, which includes further details of Callen's role (using pseudonym "Helen")
August 1950	Farrell Dobbs travels to Chicago to meet with Callen, who tells SWP how to respond to Budenz's new book
August 21, 1950	Dobbs writes letter to Cannon explaining his meeting with Callen
August 28, 1950	Cannon publishes article in the *Militant* rejecting Budenz's second book
November 16, 1953	Cannon publishes "Letter to Trotskyists Throughout the World," known as the "Open Letter"
October 7, 1954	Callen first testifies before federal grand jury investigating Soviet espionage in the US
June 18, 1958	Callen testifies before grand jury for second time
1958	Mark Zborowski found guilty of perjury for lying under oath about his ties to GPU handler Jack Soble
October 24, 1958	In a letter to Cannon, Hansen says that he tried to dissuade journalist Isaac Don Levine from stating, in his forthcoming book, that Sylvia Callen was an agent
1959	Levine publishes *The Mind of An Assassin* including Budenz's claims about Callen
March 19, 1960	Hansen responds to SLL National Secretary Gerry Healy with dishonest statements attempting to deflect Healy's interest in "Etienne," (real name Mark Zborowski) referenced by Levine
1960	Callen named as unindicted co-conspirator in indictment of GPU spy Robert Soblen, Jack Soble's brother. Soble testifies at trial about Callen's role as an agent. SWP failed to report on the issue
August 1960	Cannon writes to Rose Karsner about his political fatigue and depression
June 1963	SWP unites with Pabloite International Secretariat, forming United Secretariat

November 12, 1966	Cannon writes to Reba Hansen, Joseph Hansen's wife, regarding proposed changes to SWP Control Commission. Cannon references Callen Control Commission without mentioning her by name, stating the commission "declared the rumors unfounded"
May 1974	Nancy Fields attends IC meeting without notifying IC of her connections to CIA
August 21, 1974	James P. Cannon dies
August 1974	Workers League learns of Fields' family connections to CIA
August 31, 1974	Workers League CC votes to remove Tim Wohforth as National Secretary and suspend Fields from membership pending inquiry
September 29, 1974	Wohlforth resigns from WL
November 9, 1974	Inquiry commission report issued, uncovers that Fields' uncle, who raised her, was Albert Morris, head of the CIA's computers division and a close compatriot of Richard Helms, former CIA head, who had been a frequent visitor at Fields' home when she was growing up
March 22, 1975	WL issues statement regarding Wohforth's attacks on the party
April 1975	WRP issues statement in defense of the WL, opposing claims of "paranoia" from Joseph Hansen
May 1975	Decision to launch *Security and the Fourth International* made at Sixth Congress of the International Committee
June 5, 1975	Hansen rejects IC call for parity control commission with United Secretariat.
August 1975	David North locates and photographs Mark Zborowski in San Francisco
Early 1976	SWP publishes *James P. Cannon As We Knew Him* with fawning recollection of Sylvia Callen
January 14, 1977	Platform of Shame held in London
May 1977	David North and Alex Mitchell locate Sylvia Callen in Wheaton, Illinois
June 2, 1977	David North interviews Felix Morrow

June 20, 1977	Hansen defends SWP Control Commission, attacks WL for questioning Callen, and warns that security investigation will bring "deadly consequences"
August 1977	Alan Gelfand obtains and begins reading *Security and the FI* documents after receiving copies at SWP National Convention in Oberlin, Ohio
October 16, 1977	Tom Henehan killed at Ponce Social Club in New York City
December 1978	Gelfand files *amicus curiae* brief in support of SWP's COINTELPRO lawsuit
January 11, 1979	SWP PC votes to expel Gelfand
January 18, 1979	Joseph Hansen dies in New York City at the age of sixty-eight
January 29, 1979	Gelfand writes to SWP NC opposing his "purge" from the party
July 18, 1979	Gelfand files federal lawsuit in Los Angeles—case will become known as the Gelfand Case
November 19, 1979	First oral arguments held before US District Judge Mariana Pfaelzer in Los Angeles
June 1980	Pfaelzer denies SWP motion to dismiss lawsuit
July 1981	Angelo Torres and Edwin Sequinot convicted in Brooklyn on second-degree murder and first-degree manslaughter, respectively, for the shooting death of Tom Henehan
June 11, 1982	CIA General Counsel Stanley Sporkin writes to CIA Director William Casey citing the Gelfand Case as an "item of major interest" for the CIA
March 2–9, 1983	Gelfand trial takes place
March 9, 1983	Barnes testifies at Gelfand trial, calling Callen "one of my heroes." Pfaelzer releases Callen's 1954 and 1958 grand jury testimony
March 9, 1983	Pfaelzer announces she would rule against Gelfand
April 15, 1983	In the *Militant*, SWP leader Larry Seigle admits Budenz had also fingered Joseph Hansen as an agent, substantiating Vaughn T. O'Brien letter dated June 8, 1976
April 30, 1990	Mark Zborowski dies
January 22, 2012	Sylvia Callen dies

Glossary

Abern, Martin: (1898–1949) Founding member of the Trotskyist movement in the United States. Expelled from the Communist Party in 1928 for supporting Trotsky's struggle against the Stalinist bureaucracy. Together with Max Shachtman and James Burnham, Abern was a leader of the minority faction that opposed the characterization of the Soviet Union as a degenerated workers state, broke from the Socialist Workers Party in April 1940, and formed the Workers Party. Trotsky and Cannon criticized Abern as the leader of a petty-bourgeois clique inside the SWP.

Ageloff, Sylvia: (1910–1995) Born in New York City, Ageloff, who was employed as a social worker, was introduced to the assassin Ramon Mercader by her friend, Communist Party member Ruby Weil, on the instructions of Louis Budenz. Weil accompanied Ageloff on a trip to Europe in the summer of 1938 when the latter was traveling to attend the founding congress of the Fourth International outside Paris. It was in Europe that Ageloff first met Mercader. Ageloff then procured employment as a secretary to Trotsky in Coyoacan, and Mercader followed her, using their relationship to gain entry to the Trotsky compound. Ageloff was initially charged with murder alongside Mercader but was released by the Mexican judge overseeing the case against the protests of the prosecutor.

Barnes, Jack: (1940–) National Secretary of the Socialist Workers Party. Born in Dayton, Ohio. Conservative Republican for most of his years as a student at Carleton College. Traveled to Cuba in 1960 on a Ford Foundation grant; soon after, established contact with the Fair Play for Cuba Committee, which was heavily infiltrated by the FBI. Joined the SWP and was rapidly promoted by Joseph Hansen into the party leadership. Though the SWP never had a branch at Carleton College, a dozen of its students entered the SWP, and within a decade, occupied most key leadership positions in the organization. In the 1980s, Barnes organized the expulsion of several hundred members, including most of the older party cadre who had joined while Cannon was the party leader.

Biddle, Francis: (1886–1968) A former secretary of Supreme Court Justice Oliver Wendell Holmes Jr., Biddle served as Solicitor General under Franklin D. Roosevelt while the Justice Department prepared for the Smith Act trial. He was confirmed as Attorney General in August 1941, serving through the trial until 1945. Biddle also drew up a subversives list known as the "Biddle List" comprised of groups allegedly tied to the Communist Party. Biddle helped enforce Japanese internment during the war. He was chief American judge during the Nuremberg Trials of Nazi war criminals. In 1950, he became chairman of Americans for Democratic Action.

Booker, Lucy: Stalinist agent in whose rented New York apartment Sylvia Callen retyped SWP and Fourth International correspondence and minutes, and met with her GPU handlers Dr. Gregory Rabinowitz and Jack Soble. Booker acted as a courier for Floyd Cleveland Miller, a GPU spy in the SWP, active in the Sailors Union of the Pacific. Booker was named an unindicted co-conspirator in the Robert Soblen 1960 espionage case; she later cooperated with the FBI. In the 1930s, Booker had worked for the GPU in Germany.

Browder, Earl: (1891–1973) General Secretary of the CPUSA from 1930 to 1945. Supported Roosevelt's New Deal and promoted "Communism is 20th Century Americanism" campaign. Jailed in 1941–42 on framed-up passport violation. Expelled from CPUSA in February 1946. Worked closely with GPU in recruiting spies, especially in the preparation of Leon Trotsky's assassination.

Budenz, Louis Francis: (1891–1972) American labor activist until 1945 when he left the Communist Party and renounced socialism. Budenz, as an ex-editor of the Communist Party's *Daily Worker* and member of the party's national committee, had been personally involved in overseeing the GPU penetration of the Trotskyist movement. His two books, *This is My Story* (1947) and *Men Without Faces* (1950) exposed Stalinist infiltration of the Socialist Workers Party in great detail. These revelations shed previously unknown light on how the Stalinists orchestrated Trotsky's assassination through networks of spies in the US and Mexico. Prior to his involvement in the Communist Party, he was a leader of the Conference for Professional Labor Action (CPAC), the movement led by radical preacher AJ Muste.

Burton, John: (1953–) Lead attorney for the Gelfand Case, he conducted most of the major depositions in the litigation, including Jack Barnes, Doug Jenness, Larry Seigle, Mary-Alice Waters, Farrell Dobbs, George Novack, Vaughn T. O'Brien, Albert Glozter, Ed Heisler, Mark Zborowski, Jean van Heijenoort, Peter Camejo, and Pearl Chertov.

Callen, Sylvia: (1914–2012) Party name Caldwell, married names Franklin and Doxsee. A GPU agent operating within the Trotskyist movement who joined the movement in 1937 and worked as James P. Cannon's personal secretary in the SWP headquarters in New York from 1939 to 1947. She provided the GPU with information regarding every aspect of the SWP's political work and membership. After Max Shachtman and Albert Glotzer notified the SWP that she was an agent in March 1947, the SWP convened a purported control commission in May-June, which absolved her of blame and swore those present to secrecy. Callen then abruptly left the movement. In 1954 and 1958 she testified before federal grand juries investigating Soviet espionage. In 1958, she admitted her role as a GPU agent. This fact was not known until the transcript of the grand jury testimony was revealed through the Gelfand Case in March 1983. Jack Barnes of the SWP, testifying at the Gelfand trial, praised Callen as "one of my heroes." In 1960 she was listed as an unindicted co-conspirator in the espionage trial of GPU spy Robert Soblen. Identified as "Satyr" in the Venona Papers.

Cannon, James P. (1890–1974) Founder of the Trotskyist movement in the US. Member of the Socialist Party of America (1908); IWW (1911); founding member of the American Communist Party (1919); delegate to the Fourth (1922) and Sixth (1928) Congresses of the Communist International. In 1928, Cannon, with Maurice Spector, smuggled out Trotsky's critique of Bukharin's Draft Program, and declared support for Trotsky's struggle against the Soviet bureaucracy, thus initiating the International Left Opposition, for which he was expelled from the CP in October 1928, along with Shachtman and Abern. Co-founder of the Communist League of America (1929) and the Socialist Workers Party (1938), American section of the Fourth International. With sixteen other SWP members, jailed in 1943 for violating the 1940 Smith Act. In November 1953 Cannon authored the "Open Letter" and established the ICFI to fight Pabloism, a liquidationist pro-Stalinist trend within the Fourth International. In 1963, under the political pressures of the post-war boom, Cannon and the SWP repudiated the principles of the "Open Letter" and reunified with the Pabloite United Secretariat. Cannon's writings and speeches, especially from the 1940s, were an important contribution to Marxism. In 1968 he indicated differences with the liquidationist policies of the SWP but refrained from an open break with the party. His books include: *The Struggle for a Proletarian Party* (1943), *The History of American Trotskyism* (1944), *The First Ten Years of American Communism* (1944) and *Speeches to the Party*, a collection of speeches and articles dealing with the struggle against Pabloism. He died on August 21, 1974 in Los Angeles at the age of eighty-four. Notwithstanding his political decline in the final years of his life, James P. Cannon played a historic role in the Trotskyist movement.

Carlson, Grace: (1906–1992) Leading member of the SWP from the 1930s until 1952. Carlson, born in St. Paul, Minnesota, was one of the eighteen defendants convicted in the 1941 Smith Act trial, and was sentenced to sixteen months in prison. A former professor at the University of Minnesota, she was the party's 1940 candidate for the US Senate from Minnesota and its 1948 vice presidential candidate. She left the party in 1952 to rejoin the Catholic Church, an action which Trotskyist leader James P. Cannon ascribed to the pressures of the McCarthy-era witch-hunt and the post-World War II reaction.

Casey, William: (1913–1987) CIA Director from 1981–87, who closely followed the Gelfand Case. Casey was appointed after serving as Ronald Reagan's campaign manager in the 1980 election. Casey died within hours of being named as responsible for providing weapons to Nicaraguan extreme right-wing paramilitary contras in congressional testimony. A vicious anti-communist who advocated the "selective use of violence" against leftists, Casey was scheduled to testify to a Senate panel on the CIA's sale of weapons to Iran to fund the contras the day before he was hospitalized.

Dewey, John: (1859–1952) Noted US philosopher and educator, he wrote widely on philosophy, psychology, educational reform, and the problems of society. He was one of the founders of The New School for Social Research in New York in 1919. Deeply devoted to democratic principles and enjoying widespread respect for his integrity, Dewey took a stand against liberal and Stalinist "public opinion," and chaired the 1937 Commission of Inquiry into the Moscow Trials charges against Leon Trotsky. Known as the Dewey Commission, the exhaustive 1937 investigation exonerated Trotsky and denounced the trials as a frame-up.

Dobbs, Farrell: (1907–1983) Leader of the Minneapolis Teamsters strike in 1934. He joined the Communist League of America the same year and was elected to the national committee of the Workers Party of the United States in December. A founding member of the Socialist Workers Party in 1938, Dobbs became its national labor secretary in 1939. Dobbs was one of the eighteen members of the SWP jailed during World War II. He supported Cannon in the struggle against the Pabloite faction in the early 1950s. Later, as SWP national secretary (1953–72), Dobbs presided over the SWP's 1963 reunification with the Pabloites. In his deposition in the Gelfand Case, in 1982, he stated under oath that the SWP Political Committee had no knowledge of Hansen's 1940 meetings with the FBI. He also testified that he had no specific knowledge of the reasons Barnes was selected as his successor as national secretary of the SWP.

Dunne, Vincent Raymond (1889–1970), **Grant** (1894–1941) and **Miles** (1896–1958): Active in the Minnesota labor and socialist movement, the three Dunne brothers were expelled from the Communist Party in 1928, after solidarizing themselves with James P. Cannon and supporting Leon Trotsky and the Soviet Left Opposition. A fourth brother, William F. Dunne, remained a loyal Stalinist. Vincent, Grant and Miles joined, along with Cannon, Max Shachtman and others who had been expelled, in founding the Communist League of America. The Trotskyist Dunne brothers played major roles in the 1934 Minneapolis General Strike. They were among the defendants in the 1941 Smith Act trial. V.R. Dunne was a longtime leader of the SWP. Grant committed suicide before the trial.

FBI and State Department Officials Engaged in Hansen Communications
  George P. Shaw, Robert McGregor and **B.E. Sackett** were assigned to lead and follow the Hansen investigation. Shaw, a high-ranking State

Department diplomat, had worked at the US consulate in Tegucigalpa, Honduras; San Luis Potosi, Mexico; and Ciudad Juarez, Mexico, and was later to serve as ambassador to Nicaragua, El Salvador and Paraguay. McGregor served as secretary of the US consulate in Mexico, and Sackett was the special agent in charge of the New York division of the FBI.

Other officials following Hansen's case included **Raymond E. Murphy** of the State Department and **H.H. Clegg** of the FBI. Murphy was a well-connected State Department officer who was later to champion prosecution of suspected spy J. Alger Hiss. Murphy was the State Department official who first made information about Whittaker Chambers available to Congressman Richard M. Nixon of the House Un-American Activities Committee. Clegg was a veteran FBI agent who later served as assistant director of the FBI.

Franklin, Zalmond David (1909–1958) and **Samuel Nathan** (1882–1958): Zalmond David Franklin and his father, Samuel Nathan Franklin, both served in the Spanish Civil War. Samuel Franklin was a doctor who was elected County Coroner in Milwaukee in 1918 as a member of the Socialist Party. Long active in politics, Samuel Franklin led the Milwaukee Medical Bureau of the Stalinist-led North American Committee to Aid Spanish Democracy during the civil war. According to ship travel log records, Samuel was in Spain with the Abraham Lincoln Brigade as a medical adviser from July 1937 to February 1938. Zalmond Franklin was the second oldest of Samuel Franklin's three children. A University of Wisconsin bacteriology student, he served as an agent of the GPU in Spain from July 1937 to March 1938. Zalmond was a well-known Stalinist figure who gave public meetings throughout the Midwest on his experiences in Spain.

Gelfand, Alan: (1949–) A public defender and former member of the SWP, Gelfand obtained copies of the *Security and the Fourth International* documents at the SWP's summer conference in August 1977. Gelfand asked SWP members and leadership about the evidence of Hansen's and Callen's roles as agents, and was silenced and ultimately expelled in 1979. That year, he filed a federal lawsuit, which became known as the Gelfand Case, alleging that the US government had violated his First Amendment rights by using agents to expel him from a political party of his choosing.

Glotzer, Albert: (1908–1998) Born in the city of Pinsk, in present-day Belarus, then part of the tsarist empire. Glotzer came to the US with his family at the age of four, settling in Chicago. He joined the Young Communist League in 1923, at the age of fifteen. He soon became a leader of its successor organization, the Young Workers League, and was expelled from the Communist Party and the youth movement in 1928, along with other Trotskyists who would form the Communist League of America. In 1931 Glotzer spent weeks as a secretary and guard for Leon Trotsky, then exiled in Prinkipo, Turkey. Glotzer became a close ally of Max Shachtman in many of the internal disputes within the American Trotskyist movement. Refusing to defend the USSR against imperialism, Glotzer split from the SWP as part of the petty-bourgeois opposition in 1940. In 1947, he and Shachtman visited SWP headquarters to notify the party of Sylvia Callen's role as a GPU agent. He later followed Shachtman in moving sharply to the right, joining the Democratic Party and defending the crimes of American imperialism in Cuba and Vietnam.

Goldman, Albert: (1897–1960) Goldman became a lawyer in 1925 and joined the Communist Party in the late 1920s. Expelled from the CP for his criticisms of the Soviet Union, which he visited in 1930, he joined the Trotskyist CLA in 1933. The following year, he left the CLA to join the Socialist Party, reuniting with the Trotskyists when they entered the Socialist Party in 1936. In 1938, he was elected to the SWP national committee, and served as Trotsky's US attorney. Goldman was chief defense counsel as well as one of the defendants in the 1941 Minneapolis trial. While still in prison he formed a right-wing faction with Felix Morrow. He left the SWP and joined Shachtman's Workers Party, from which he resigned in 1949.

GPU: (*Gosudarstvennoe Politicheskoe Upravleniie*) The State Political Administration, i.e., the Soviet secret police, later known as the NKVD and KGB. The GPU was provided with extensive funds and resources to assassinate Trotsky (1940), his son Leon Sedov (1938) and many other leading members of the Fourth International.

Hansen, Joseph: (1910–1979) A GPU agent inside the American Trotskyist movement who, after Trotsky's assassination, offered his services as an informer to the FBI. Hansen joined the Trotskyist movement in 1934 from Salt Lake City and moved to San Francisco where he worked on the seamen's union newspaper, *Voice of Federation*. He later edited *Labor Action*, the Trotskyist weekly produced in California. In 1937, he became a secretary to Trotsky in

Mexico. When Trotsky was assassinated in August 1940, Hansen offered his services to FBI officials in Mexico City. On his return to the US, Hansen, a member of the SWP national committee, made contact with FBI officials in New York. A document uncovered by the International Committee in 1983 revealed that Hansen had been identified by ex-Stalinist leader Louis Budenz as a GPU agent. Hansen edited the *Militant* and, with his wife Reba, established *World Outlook*, later *Intercontinental Press*. He was responsible for the international relations of the SWP during the 1950s and 1960s, and led the party after Cannon's retirement. He was a determined advocate of reunification with the Pabloites in 1963. During the 1960s, Hansen supervised the recruitment and training of a group of Carleton College students who took over leadership of the SWP.

Harte, Robert Sheldon: (1915–1940) A GPU agent recruited from the Communist Party to infiltrate the Trotskyist movement, Harte served as Trotsky's guard in Coyoacan and opened the compound gate for the assassination team led by painter David Alfaro Siqueiros on May 24, 1940. Harte either left with the assassination team or was abducted by them. Several weeks later, his body was discovered after the Siqueiros team had executed him. A photo of Stalin was discovered in his New York apartment, and he was listed as an agent in the Venona Papers.

Healy, Gerry: (1913–1989) Principal leader of the Trotskyist movement following World War II. His drift toward Pabloite positions, particularly in relation to bourgeois national movements, became increasingly pronounced in the mid-1970s, following the founding of the Workers Revolutionary Party.

Henehan, Tom: (1951–1977) Born in Kalamazoo, Michigan, Tom joined the Workers League in New York City in the spring of 1973. He became a leader of the Young Socialists, worked as a printer for the party, and was active among the miners and at the Navy dockyards. On October 16, 1977, Tom was gunned down at the Ponce Social Club by professional gunmen. The Workers League carried out a vigorous campaign to bring his killers to justice. Speaking in 1997, twenty years after his death, David North said: "Even after twenty years, so many facets of his personality remain vivid in our memories of Tom: his intelligence, determination, physical courage, compassion, energy, sense of humor and enthusiastic enjoyment of life."

Hook, Sidney: (1902–1989) Student of John Dewey at Columbia University and noted pragmatist. In the 1930s Hook was sympathetic to Marxism, which he claimed could be reconciled with pragmatic thought. After World War II, Hook became an anti-communist social democrat, supported the cold war and polemicized against Marxism, particularly in the field of philosophy. He was professor of philosophy at New York University from 1927to 1972.

Hoover, J. Edgar: (1895–1972) Director of the Federal Bureau of Investigation (and its predecessor, the Bureau of Investigation) from 1924 until his death. Before leading federal law enforcement, Hoover was head of the Radical Division of the Bureau of Investigation and oversaw the Palmer Raid round-ups and deportations of socialists and anarchists. He closely followed the infiltration of the Trotskyist movement in the 1930s, 1940s and beyond. As architect of the Counter Intelligence Program (COINTELPRO), Hoover organized illegal surveillance and infiltration of socialist, civil rights and anti-war groups.

Kluger, Pearl: (1912–2001) According to Vaughn T. O'Brien, Kluger was in the American Workers Party with A.J. Muste and Louis Budenz, and later was a secretary for the American Committee for the Defense of Leon Trotsky. "In the late '40s or early '50s," O'Brien recounted, Kluger told him that "Budenz says your friend Joe Hansen worked with the GPU."

Levine, Isaac Don: (1892–1981) A writer of Belorussian origin, Levine moved to the United States in 1911. Abandoning his earlier support for socialism, Levine became the editor of the anti-communist magazine *Plain Talk* after World War Two. Levine had intricate knowledge of the workings of the world Stalinist operations, having collaborated with the defector Walter Krivitsky and ex-CP member Whittaker Chambers in preparing their defections from Stalinism. Levine testified to the House Un-American Activities Committee against Alger Hiss in 1948. Later, he corresponded with Joseph Hansen in preparation for his book on the GPU murder of Trotsky in his 1960 book *The Mind of An Assassin*. Levine appeared as an interviewee in the 1981 film *Reds*.

Mercader del Rio, Ramon (Frank Jacson/Jacques Mornard): (1913–1978) Stalinist agent who assassinated Leon Trotsky in Mexico in August 1940. Born in Barcelona, the son of a Catalonian Stalinist, he fought in the Spanish

Civil War. On his release from a Mexican prison in 1960, he was welcomed in Cuba, and then, in 1961, in the Soviet Union, which awarded him the Order of Lenin for his murder of Trotsky. In 1977 the International Committee obtained information that Mercader was living in the Soviet Union. In 1978 it was reported that he had died in Cuba.

The *Militant*: First English language newspaper of the Trotskyist movement, appearing November 15, 1928, following the expulsion of Cannon and Shachtman from the CPUSA. Renamed the *New Militant* after fusion with the American Workers Party in December 1934; ended publication after the Trotskyists entered the Socialist Party in June 1936. After expulsion from the Socialist Party in August 1937, the US Trotskyists published *Socialist Appeal*, the name given to the internal journal they produced inside the SP. The paper was renamed the *Militant* in February 1941.

Mink, George: (1899–1940) Mink was a GPU agent, notorious for his brutality and suspected of numerous killings on behalf of the Stalinist police. In the late 1930s, reports surfaced that the GPU had decided to liquidate Mink. After Hansen made contact with the FBI, Hoover instructed his agents to question Hansen about reports that he had participated in Mink's murder in Mexico. Mink's body was never discovered, and no one knows for sure what became of him.

Minneapolis General Strike: (1934) Mass strike action from May 18–28, organized by Trotskyist leaders of the Teamsters local, including unemployed and unorganized workers, forced over 160 employers to recognize Local 574 as a bargaining agent. In June, employers broke this agreement, and Roosevelt's labor board intervened. When workers struck in mid-July, the police shot pickets, killing two and injuring scores, in order to force National Guard involvement. The ensuing five-week strike forced employers to concede the union's main demands. This campaign, which used new tactics, including flying squads of pickets and other mass action, won nationwide recognition for the Trotskyist movement among American workers, and was a catalyst for the formation of industrial unions in the US.

Mitchell, Alex: (1942–) Mitchell was a highly-respected investigative journalist in Britain prior to joining the Socialist Labour League in 1971. Subsequently became editor of the *Workers Press*, and later the *News Line*.

He played a leading role in the early stages of the *Security and the Fourth International* investigtion. He supported Healy during the 1985–86 crisis within the WRP, broke with the International Committee, and returned to Australia where he resumed his career as a journalist.

Morrow, Felix: (1905–1992) A founding member of the SWP, Morrow was a member of the Political Committee from the late 1930s until his expulsion in 1946, when he moved to the right. In a June, 1977 interview, Morrow told David North that the SWP never authorized Hansen's contact with the FBI following the assassination of Trotsky.

Moscow Trials: (1936–1938) In the course of three frame-up trials, leading members of Lenin's politburo were falsely accused and convicted of crimes against the USSR. These included charges of economic sabotage, spying for imperialist powers and organizing anti-Soviet terrorist activity. Trotsky and his son, Leon Sedov, the major defendants in the trials, were found guilty *in absentia*. In 1988 all the defendants of the Moscow Trials, except for Trotsky and his son, were rehabilitated. The Dewey Commission, led by the American philosopher John Dewey, condemned the trials as frame-ups.

Muste, Abraham Johannes: (1885–1967) Protestant minister and pacifist, Muste, the son of Dutch immigrants, founded the Conference for Progressive Labor Action in 1929 and then organized the American Workers Party (AWP) in 1933. The AWP fused with the Communist League of America in 1934 to form the Workers Party of the United States. Muste returned to the church in the summer of 1936. He was prominent in the movement against the Vietnam War in the 1960s.

News Line: The daily organ of the WRP from 1976 to 1985.

North, David: (1950–) Joined the Trotskyist movement in 1971, and was elected national secretary of the Workers League in 1976. He played a leading role in the International Committee's investigation into the assassination of Leon Trotsky, writing many of the key documents associated with *Security and the Fourth International*. Between 1982 and 1985 North developed an extensive written critique of Healy and the WRP. Following the 1995 transformation of the Workers League into the Socialist Equality Party, North remained national secretary. At the official founding congress of the Socialist Equality

Party in 2008, North was elected national chairman. He also holds the post of chairman of the international editorial board of the World Socialist Web Site. Author of *The Heritage We Defend, In Defense of Leon Trotsky, The Russian Revolution and the Unfinished Twentieth Century*, and numerous books, essays and major political documents of the Fourth International.

O'Brien, Vaughn T.: (1910–1995) a close personal friend of Joseph Hansen from Utah; guard to Trotsky in Coyoacan. In June 1976, he wrote a letter to Hansen, purporting to give an account of Hansen's meetings with the GPU in 1938. His account contradicted that given by Hansen in *Healy's Big Lie*. O'Brien's wife told Harold Robins, "They made up the story out of the whole cloth."

Pfaelzer, Mariana: (1926–2015) Appointed to the US District Court for the Central District of California by Jimmy Carter in 1978, Pfaelzer presided over the Gelfand Case and allowed the case to go to trial. Previously, she was president of the Los Angeles Police Commission from 1976 to 1978. In 1994, Pfaelzer attracted national attention by ruling that Proposition 187—a California ballot initiative that denied welfare, healthcare and public school access to undocumented immigrants—was unconstitutional.

Poyntz, Juliet Stuart: (1886–1937) Member of the American Communist Party who disappeared under mysterious circumstances in 1937. Poyntz was born in Omaha, Nebraska, studied at Barnard College in New York and joined the Socialist Party and, after the October 1917 Revolution in Russia, the newly-formed American Communist Party. She later left the CP, according to those who knew her, in order to work for Soviet intelligence. Poyntz traveled to Moscow in 1936, at the time of the first of the infamous Moscow Trials. Apparently disillusioned and angered by what she had seen in the USSR, she returned to the US, where she disappeared in June 1937, a victim of a Stalinist assassination squad. In 1938, Carlo Tresca accused the Stalinist regime of killing Poyntz, saying that she had told him of her disgust and disillusionment with Stalinism.

Rabinowitz, Dr. Gregory: (A.k.a. "Roberts" and "John") Top GPU spymaster in the US, responsible for recruiting agents in the plot to murder Leon Trotsky. Beginning in late 1936 and early 1937, he instructed Louis Budenz to find agents to infiltrate the Trotskyist movement in the US. Among the agents he recruited were Sylvia Callen and F.C. Miller.

Schweinhaut, Henry Albert (1902–1970) and **Berge, Wendell** (1903–1955): Henry A. Schweinhaut and Wendell Berge led the prosecution of twenty-eight SWP members during the Smith Act trial of 1941. In 1944, Roosevelt appointed Schweinhaut judge of the US District Court for the District of Columbia, a post he occupied until his death. In 1930 Berge worked in the Justice Department's antitrust division before Roosevelt appointed him as Assistant Attorney General in charge of the Department of Justice's criminal division in 1941. In 1943, Berge transferred to Assistant Attorney General overseeing the antitrust division.

Shachtman, Max: (1904–1972) Founding member of the American Trotskyist movement in 1928, after he, Cannon, and Abern were expelled from the CP for supporting Trotsky. Shachtman translated and published Trotsky's works; he wrote the important exposure *Behind the Moscow Trials.* He wrote for the *Militant,* and, from 1923, edited the *New International.* In 1939–40, after the Stalin-Hitler Pact, he led the petty-bourgeois opposition in the SWP, together with James Burnham. After his expulsion in April 1940, Shachtman organized the Workers Party, and from 1949, the Independent Socialist League, claiming that the Soviet bureaucracy had become a new ruling class. He moved steadily to the right, and supported imperialist intervention in Korea and Vietnam. In 1958, he dissolved his organization into the Socialist Party, joining that organization's right wing, and becoming an adviser to the anti-communist AFL-CIO.

Siqueiros, David Alfaro: (1896–1974) Mexican muralist, devoted Stalinist and GPU agent. On May 24, 1940, he led the GPU assassination attempt at Trotsky's house in Coyoacan. Twenty thugs disguised as police invaded the house with machine guns and firebombs. Admitted at the front gate by Robert Sheldon Harte—a Stalinist agent who had infiltrated the Trotskyist movement—the murder squad fired hundreds of bullets directly into Trotsky's bedroom. However, Trotsky and his wife, Natalia Sedova, escaped injury.

Skoglund, Carl: (1884–1960) Emigrated from Sweden to the US in 1911. Skoglund had been active in the socialist movement in Sweden, and continued his political activity in the US. Skoglund was among the Trotskyists expelled from the Communist Party by the American Stalinists in 1928. He played a leading role in the 1934 Minneapolis General Strike, and was also among the Minneapolis Smith Act defendants in 1941. The US government later tried to deport Skoglund to Sweden, and the persecution placed severe limitations on his public trade union and political activity. Skoglund lived his final years at the Socialist Workers Party educational camp, and died there in 1960.

Soble, Jack: (1903–1967) Born Abromas Soblevicius, party name Adolph Senin. Of Lithuanian background, Senin was active in the German Communist Party and integrated himself into the Trotskyist movement, visiting Trotsky in Prinkipo in 1931 and Copenhagen in 1932. He arrived in the US in 1941 where he continued his work as an agent and served as the primary GPU handler for Sylvia Callen. Arrested for espionage in 1957 with his wife, Myra Soble, and convicted. In 1961, Soble testified against his brother, GPU ringleader Robert Soblen. In December 1932, Trotsky, suspicious of Senin, had broken with him: "You will one day regret what you are doing. I never want to see you again."

Soblen, Robert: (1900–1962) Born Ruvelis Sobolevicius, party name Roman Well, Soblen infiltrated the party and, alongside his brother, Jack Soble, played a deliberately disruptive role in the movement on the orders of the GPU. Senin moved to the United States in 1941. When he was indicted in 1960, Callen was listed as an unindicted co-conspirator. Soblen was convicted for espionage and, after attempting to escape to Israel, committed suicide while being deported to the US.

Socialist Workers Party (SWP): American section of the Fourth International (1938–1963), whose founding conference was held from December 31, 1937 to January 3, 1938. Trotsky played a central role in the programmatic preparation of the conference. Its origins lay in the 1928 expulsion of Cannon, Abern, and Shachtman from the CP for supporting Trotsky. They formed the Communist League of America (CLA) (1929–34); fused with Muste's group to form the Workers Party of the US (1934–36); entered into the Socialist Party and won over its youth movement (1936–37), to win the forces to found the SWP. The leading party of the Fourth International, it played a key political role over the next two decades. In November 1953 the SWP, under Cannon's leadership, published the "Open Letter" and initiated the formation of the International Committee of the Fourth International (ICFI) to fight Pabloite revisionism. In the mid-1950s, however, the SWP began to repudiate its Trotskyist heritage. This culminated in its reunification with the

Pabloites in 1963, and its split from Trotskyism. The Workers League/SEP has its origins in a minority tendency which opposed this betrayal. The SWP's political degeneration was associated with the rise of Joseph Hansen into the top leadership and large-scale FBI infiltration of the organization.

Stalin-Hitler pact: (1939) Signed by Molotov and Ribbentrop on August 23, 1939. The pact provided for carving up Poland between Germany and the USSR. Secret protocols provided Soviet control of Latvia, Estonia, Bessarabia, and Lithuania, the latter in exchange for payment of 7.5 million gold dollars or 31.5 million German marks. Stalin scrupulously observed the terms of the pact, delivering oil, wheat and metals into Germany until June 22, the day Hitler invaded the USSR in "Operation Barbarossa." Stalin had systematically disarmed the Red Army and left the USSR totally unprepared for war, despite repeated warnings; within the first two weeks of the invasion, the Nazis killed several million people. Ultimately, an estimated 25 million Soviets died during the brutal war.

Stein, Morris: (Morris Lewit) (1903–1998) A CP member from a young age, he joined the Trotskyist CLA in 1930 and became a national committee member of the Workers Party of the United States in 1934, and acting SWP national secretary after the US government jailed eighteen SWP leaders in 1943. In the postwar period he was national organizational secretary and played a prominent role in the struggle against the Pabloite tendency in 1953. He withdrew from political activity in the early 1960s.

Third International: Established in March 1919 under the leadership of Lenin and Trotsky to organize the world socialist revolution after the betrayal and collapse of the Second International. The work of the first four congresses (1919–1922) of the Communist International (Comintern), held when Lenin and Trotsky still led the Soviet Union, made an immense contribution to the development of revolutionary strategy and tactics. The Comintern degenerated into a tool of Stalinist foreign policy by the late 1920s. It held its last Congress in 1935 and was officially dissolved by Stalin in 1943.

Thomas, Norman: (1884–1968) A Presbyterian minister, he was moved by "grotesque inequalities, conspicuous waste, gross exploitation and unnecessary poverty" to leave the church in 1918 and declare himself a socialist. He was one of the founders of the American Civil Liberties Union. He assumed leadership of the American Socialist Party in 1926. Thomas was a well-known orator and ran six times for the presidency (1928–48), receiving one million votes in the 1932 election.

Tobin, Daniel J.: (1875–1955) President of the International Brotherhood of Teamsters (IBT) from 1907–52. Conservative Irish Catholic and anti-communist, he opposed the formation of mass industrial unions and favored craft unions. Ardent "New-Dealer" and backer of President Franklin Roosevelt and the Democratic Party. Tobin worked with the FBI-led opposition within Minneapolis IBT Local 544 to depose its SWP leaders. After Local 544 members voted to join the nascent CIO, Tobin sent a telegram to Roosevelt on June 12, 1941 to urge prosecution of its leaders as advocating disruption of national trucking and the overthrow of the government, in time of (impending) war. During WWII, he enforced a no-strike pledge.

Tresca, Carlo: (1879–1943) Italian-American journalist, speaker and anarchist organizer who emigrated to the US in 1904. Tresca joined the Industrial Workers of the World in 1912 and played an active role in strikes in Lawrence, Massachusetts; Paterson, New Jersey and the Mesabi iron range of northern Minnesota. He was a bitter opponent of the fascist regime of Benito Mussolini, and fought against Mussolini's Italian-American supporters. In the 1930s he denounced the Stalinist terror in the Soviet Union and served on the Dewey Commission in 1937, which found Leon Trotsky not guilty of the Stalinist frame-up charges that had been leveled against him. Tresca was murdered in lower Manhattan in January 1943, the work of a Stalinist assassination squad.

Trotsky, Lev Davidovich: (1879–1940) Alongside Lenin, the greatest revolutionary Marxist of the twentieth century and founder of the Fourth International. Joined the revolutionary movement in 1898. Collaborated with Lenin on *Iskra* in London 1902–03. Leader of the St. Petersburg Soviet in 1905. Joined the Bolshevik Party in 1917. Chief organizer of the October 1917 insurrection, first Commissar for Foreign Affairs, head of the Soviet Red Army (1918–25). In 1923, he formed the Left Opposition to fight the developing Soviet bureaucracy. He was expelled from the CPSU in 1927 and exiled to Turkey in 1929. In 1933, he called for the formation of a new communist international. In preparation, he wrote *The Revolution Betrayed: What is the Soviet Union and Where is it Going?* and *The Transitional Program*, the founding document of the Fourth International in 1938. He was assassinated in Mexico on Stalin's orders by GPU agent Ramon Mercader in August 1940.

United Secretariat of the Fourth International: (USFI; USEC) Formed by the unprincipled reunification between the SWP and the Pabloite International Secretariat in 1963. Led by Ernest Mandel, the USEC fostered illusions in the Stalinist bureaucracy, bourgeois nationalists and the trade union and labor bureaucracies. The 1963 unity with the SWP proved extremely unstable, as each group often lined up with opposing bourgeois movements and politicians. In 1974 and in 1982–84, Joseph Hansen and his successor Jack Barnes expelled Mandel supporters from the SWP. In June 1990, the SWP broke off all political relations with the USFI. In the late 1980s, the USFI promoted Gorbachev and backed his program of capitalist restoration, declaring him one of the greatest political figures of the twentieth century. In 1989–91, the USFI supported the restoration of capitalism in Eastern Europe, the nationalist breakup of Yugoslavia, and the "right" of the Croatian fascists and other extreme right-wing nationalists to establish their own state institutions.

Weil, Ruby: (est. b. 1904) Born in Evansville, Indiana. An undercover member of the CPUSA, she was recruited by Louis Budenz to introduce Trotsky supporter Sylvia Ageloff to Ramon Mercader, alias Jacques Mornard in Paris in 1938, around the time of the founding of the Fourth International. Ruby's sister Marian Weil was also an ardent Stalinist.

Weissman, Susan: (1949–) Professor at St. Mary's College of California from 1992 and author of books on Victor Serge. An ardent Pabloite, she supported the expulsion of Alan Gelfand from the SWP and endorsed the SWP's obstruction of Gelfand's attempts to compel GPU agents Sylvia Callen and Mark Zborowski to testify under oath in 1981–83. Weissman was later a member of Solidarity, and beginning in 1986 served on the editorial board of its paper, *Against the Current.*

Weissman wrote a series summarizing the known evidence concerning Zborowski, which denounced the *Security and the Fourth International* investigation as a "bizarre, sectarian smear campaign."

Wohlforth, Tim: (1933–) Joined Shachtman's youth group, the Socialist Youth League (SYL) in 1953, and the SWP in 1957. He led the pro-ICFI minority inside the SWP (1961–64) and in 1964 was expelled from the SWP with eight others, for demanding a discussion on the LSSP's 1964 betrayal in Sri Lanka. Founding member of the Workers League in 1966. Disoriented by the decline of the anti-war protest movement, Wohlforth's behavior as national secretary assumed an increasingly erratic, personally irresponsible, and politically destructive character. Wohlforth deserted the Workers League in 1974, after concealing the CIA family connections of his companion, **Nancy Fields**. He rejoined the SWP, being briefly elevated to its political committee. In 1993, he issued a public call for imperialist intervention in Bosnia in a notorious article titled, "Give War a Chance." In 1994 he endorsed the US invasion of Haiti. In the 1990s, he denounced the Trotskyist movement as a "cult," abandoned socialist politics, and took up the writing of crime novels.

Workers League: US Trotskyist party, from 1995, the Socialist Equality Party. Founded in 1966 by members of the American Committee for the Fourth International, in solidarity with the ICFI, after their 1964 expulsion from the SWP for demanding a discussion on the betrayal of Trotskyism by the Sri Lankan LSSP. The Workers League published the *Bulletin*, later the *International Workers Bulletin*. It is succeeded by the SEP and its international online publication, the World Socialist Web Site, published from 1998 onwards.

Workers Revolutionary Party: (WRP) In 1973, led by Healy, Banda and Slaughter, the Trotskyist SLL transformed itself into the WRP, without international discussion among the ICFI sections. From the outset, its foundation was based on a reformist program: "to unite the working class behind a socialist program to throw out the Tory government and replace it with a Labour government." Over the next decade, the WRP degenerated into a national opportunist formation that broke apart and split from the ICFI in 1985–86. In 1986, the genuine Trotskyists inside the WRP formed the International Communist Party (ICP), the British section of the ICFI, now the Socialist Equality Party. The WRP published the *News Line*, expressly supporting bourgeois nationalism, from 1976 on.

Wright, John G.: (Joseph "Usick" Vanzler) (1901–1956) Joined the Trotskyist CLA in 1933; founding member of the SWP; National Committee member from 1939–56. One of Trotsky's closest intellectual collaborators, Wright translated many of Trotsky's writings into English from Russian and French, making them available to a broad public. He played a leading role in the SWP during the 1940s and 1950s. He contributed numerous articles on Soviet affairs and theoretical questions until his death in 1956.

Zborowski, Mark: (1908–1990) In 1934, under the assumed name "Etienne," the GPU agent wormed his way into the Fourth International in Paris, becoming the confidante of Trotsky's son Lev Sedov. His information assisted the GPU in November 1936 to steal part of Trotsky's archives from the Nicolaevsky Institute. He assisted in the murder of Lev Sedov (February 1938), of Trotsky's secretaries Erwin Wolf (July 1937) and Rudolph Klement (August 1938), and of supporters including Ignatz Reiss (September 1937). He was the "Russian delegate" at the founding conference of the FI in September 1938. He was instrumental in the plot to assassinate Leon Trotsky. In 1941, Lola Dallin brought him out of Vichy France to the US, where he continued to spy as part of the Soble ring. He was convicted in 1958 for perjury, appealed, and convicted after retrial in 1962. Despite this, he enjoyed a comfortable career as an anthropologist. In August 1975, David North located him in San Francisco and photographed him. During the Gelfand Case, the SWP opposed his deposition, which nonetheless took place on April 15, 1982; there Zborowski "took the Fifth" and refused to testify. Judge Pfaelzer blocked his testimony on the grounds that it might expose US government agents.